Gary McIndoe is founder and managing director of Latitude Law Solicitors. He has over 30 years' experience in immigration practice, across both publicly-funded and private sectors, and is a former director of Greater Manchester Immigration Aid Unit. Gary is a trustee of Manchester-based refugee advocacy organisation RAPAR, and Chair of the Electronic Immigration Network, a charity providing online information in the field of immigration and asylum. He is listed as a leading individual by Chambers and Partners and the Legal 500.

Gemma Tracey is an associate at Latitude Law, where she has worked since it formed in 2007. She has particular expertise in preparing family applications, deportation appeals, nationality applications and sponsor licensing. She was shortlisted for 'Legal Professional of the Year' at the Manchester Young Talent Awards 2018, and 'Lawyer of the Year' at the Made in Manchester Awards 2019.

Deportation – A Practical Guide

Deportation – A Practical Guide

Gary McIndoe

Gemma Tracey

Law Brief Publishing

Published 2021 by Law Brief Publishing, an imprint of Law Brief Publishing Ltd
30 The Parks
Minehead
Somerset
TA24 8BT

www.lawbriefpublishing.com

Paperback: 978-1-913715-16-8

PREFACE

This practical guide to challenging deportation decisions was conceived during the UK's first lockdown in 2020, and drafted over the following 10 months, taking in the end of the Brexit implementation period and a seismic change in how the deportation of EU citizens will be managed henceforth. The law is as stated on 1 May 2021.

Gary McIndoe
Gemma Tracey
May 2021

CONTENTS

INTRODUCTION

Every sovereign state has the right to regulate the entry and residence of non-citizens. Even where an element of sovereignty has been ceded – for example, through membership of an international organisation such as the European Union – the state retains an ultimate power to examine, and if felt appropriate exclude, certain individuals from its territory.

The power to deport someone is the most draconian expression of this sovereign right. It is important from the outset to recognise that the word "deport" is a term of art in British law. It doesn't simply mean removal or sending someone to another country – it means removal *and exclusion* from the UK, potentially forever. Permanent separation from family and friends here. In this book we will examine the way in which the nation's power to deport those who are not its citizens – and in extreme cases even some who have acquired British citizenship – has developed in the modern era. How the state uses its statutory powers, and how best to head off or challenge a decision to deport your client.

The earliest legislation that remains relevant today is the Immigration Act 1971. Coming into force on 1 January 1973 under the Conservative government of Edward Heath, and following hot on the heels of Harold Wilson's Labour Commonwealth Immigrants Act in 1968, this Act contained what remains today the cornerstone of the British state's power to deport people from its shores.

There have been many further pieces of legislation enacted since 1973, attempting variously to tighten the UK's rules on deportation, and on occasion to direct precisely how decision-makers including tribunals and court should interpret principles of human rights law. In early 2021 we seem to have reached a turning point in the judicial approach to deportation decisions; the deference of recent years has given way to a more interventionist approach which, from a practitioner's point of view, is to be welcomed. On the horizon, however, are reforms to judicial review (in England and Wales at least) which stand to curb the ability of the judiciary to supervise how the executive uses its powers, includes those to deport individuals who are present here.

CHAPTER ONE

EXERCISE OF POWERS UNDER THE IMMIGRATION ACT 1971

The Immigration Act 1971 received Royal Assent on 28 October 1971, but the majority of the Act didn't come into force until 1 January 1973. The Act includes various provisions in relation to the deportation of those who are not British. It confirms that, in order to deport a non-British person from the UK, the Secretary of State must be persuaded that their (or a member of their family's) deportation from the UK is conducive to the public good (s3(5)). In addition, deportation can also be pursued if a court recommends an individual who is over the age of 17 for deportation; in such cases, the individual must have been convicted of an offence punishable with imprisonment (s3(6)).

No definition of the phrase "conducive to the public good" was included in the 1971 Act. However, section 32(4) of the UK Borders Act 2007, discussed further in Chapter 3, took a step in that direction by setting out circumstances in which a person's deportation was "deemed to be conducive to the public good".

Until the Human Rights Act 1998 came into force on 2 October 2000, deportation was more widely used as a method of removing individuals from the UK. Section 3(5) and 3(6) decisions were routinely made against overstayers and illegal entrants, rather than just in respect of those with criminal convictions. You may still see clients who were subject to a deportation order before October 2000, in respect of whom it is relatively straightforward to seek revocation on the ground that – under the current legislative framework – they would never have been made the subject of a deportation decision.

Turning to cases involving criminality, where a court recommends deportation, the offender must be given at least seven days' notice in writing (s6(2)), and the only way the offender can challenge the court's recommendation is if the offender appeals against the sentence imposed.

The Secretary of State will not be able to issue a deportation order while the appeal proceedings are pending (s6(6)). Whether an offence is punishable with imprisonment will be determined without any regard to the fact that the offender is a young offender, a first offender, or hasn't previously been sentenced to imprisonment (s6(3)(b)). This means that the court could recommend an offender for deportation without actually imposing a custodial sentence, just as long as the offender has been convicted of an offence which is punishable with imprisonment. In our experience, criminal courts rarely recommend deportation nowadays, and the Secretary of State usually pursues deportation cases with reference to s3(5) of the Immigration Act 1971. A criminal court's power to recommend an individual for deportation is usually reserved for the most serious criminal matters.

Section 5 of the 1971 Act provides further information in relation to the procedure the Secretary of State must follow when considering the deportation of a non-British national from the UK. Section 5(1) clarifies that if a person is liable to deportation under s3(5) or 3(6), the Secretary of State **may** issue a deportation order, thus confirming that discretion exists; issuing a deportation order is by no means mandatory under the 1971 Act. If issued, a deportation order will require the person to leave the UK, and it prohibits them from returning. The order will invalidate any existing leave that the person held prior to the order being made, and whilst in force, a person cannot secure any leave to remain. This means that a person who is the subject of a deportation order would need to revoke the order before being in a position to receive a grant of leave to enter or remain; s5(2) confirms that the order may be revoked at any time, and that the order would cease to have effect if the individual becomes a British citizen. Obviously, it would be very beneficial to prove that an individual is in fact British or is entitled to register as such, so practitioners should first consider this option. If the individual has no claim to British citizenship, revocation should be considered (see Chapter 7 of this guide). Bear in mind, also, that you can apply to revoke a deportation order without the individual having left the UK under the terms of that order.

As noted above, in addition to deporting an offender, the Secretary of State also has powers to deport the offender's family. Section 5(3), however, confirms that if seeking to deport family members the Secretary of State must issue the deportation order to the family no more than 8 weeks after the deportation order against the main offender has been issued. Understandably, the deportation order will cease to have effect if the family relationship breaks down, or if the deportation order against the main offender ceases to have effect. Section 5(4) defines a family member in this context.

Section 5 confirms that Schedule 3 of the Act shall have effect with respect to the removal and detention of those facing deportation. Schedule 3 confirms that the Secretary of State may give directions to remove those liable to deportation to a country of which they are a national or citizen, or to a country or territory where there is reason to believe the individual will be admitted (s1(1), Schedule 3). Schedule 3 also confirms the Secretary of State's powers in relation to detention; those recommended for deportation may be detained pending the making of an order from the Secretary of State, or whilst the order is in force. Detention shall continue unless the individual is released on immigration bail under Schedule 10 to the Immigration Act 2016 (s2(3)). The remainder of Schedule 3 is no longer in force, having been repealed by the Immigration Act 2016.

If an individual who is liable to deportation under s3(5) or 3(6) permanently leaves the UK before a deportation order has been made, they may be able to claim financial support from the Secretary of State to cover the expenses incurred in leaving the UK (s5(6)).

CHAPTER TWO

WHO IS EXEMPT FROM DEPORTATION?

Is my client British?

As it would significantly assist if your client is British, this is the first question to ask when advising clients in deportation cases.

It is beyond the scope of this book to consider the provisions of the British Nationality Act 1981 in depth, but the following points should be noted:

- All those born in the UK prior to the commencement of the 1981 Act on 1 January 1983 acquired British citizenship by birth regardless of their or their parents' status in the UK.

- Under section 1(3) of the 1981 Act a person born in the UK after commencement will be British if, at the time of birth, their father or mother is British or is settled. If the individual's father is British or settled and the individual was born before 1 July 2016, the father must have been married to the child's mother at the time of birth. If the parents weren't married and the mother wasn't British/settled at the time of birth, the child will not acquire British citizenship at birth, but is entitled to register as British.

- A person born abroad to a parent who is a British citizen *otherwise than by descent* will themselves be a British citizen by descent.

If your entitlement to citizenship is automatic, past criminality will not pose a problem. If you are required to register as British, the "good character" requirement that applies to the vast majority of citizenship applicants can lead to the refusal of an application.

However, in October 2016 the Supreme Court handed down judgment in the case of **R (on the application of Johnson) v Secretary of State for the Home Department [2016] UKSC 56**, which considered registration applications under the aforementioned section 4F of the British Nationality Act 1981. Under s4F, individuals are entitled to register as British citizens if the sole reason they can't register under other provisions of the Act (s1(3), s3(2), s3(5), paragraph 4 Schedule 2 or paragraph 5 Schedule 2) is because their mother wasn't married to their father at the time of birth. Initially, the Secretary of State required such individuals to meet the good character requirement, which of course could prevent, or significantly delay the submission of, applications from those with a criminal record. However, in **Johnson**, the Supreme Court determined that, whilst it is reasonable to expect such individuals to have to apply to register as British, it is not reasonable to impose the additional hurdle of a good character test. Therefore, regardless of their criminal record, such individuals can register as British citizens.

In the subsequent case of **R(Bangs) v Secretary of State for the Home Department** this principle was taken further. The applicant here had been born in the 1960s to a British mother and an American father. When he was born, he was not eligible for British citizenship as the law at the time did not allow a British mother to pass on her nationality. Mr Bangs was convicted of murder in 1993 and released on life licence in 2004. He was then convicted in 2013 of an offence of using threatening words, for which he received a fine of £150. The Home Office initiated deportation proceedings against him. The applicant made a human rights claim which was certified under s94B of the Nationality, Immigration and Asylum Act 2002 meaning that he could not appeal against the decision to refuse his claim from inside the UK. He challenged this decision.

Under section 4C of the British Nationality Act 1981, a person became entitled to be registered as British where they were born before 1 January 1983 and their mother is British. This provision came into force on 30 April 2003. Since 13 January 2010, a person applying under this route also had to satisfy the good character requirement. Due to his criminal convictions, Mr Bangs could not satisfy the good character requirement under s4C and so was not eligible for British citizenship. As such, he argued that the good character requirement in the context of s4C was incompatible with his Article 8 rights.

By a consent order, sealed on 04 July 2017, the High Court made an order quashing the deportation and s94B certification decisions. The court held that the good character requirement in s4C is incompatible with Article 8 of the European Convention on Human Rights.

The good character requirement remains in place for those seeking to acquire British citizenship under discretionary provisions in the 1981 Act; serious criminality will therefore make it impossible to become British in order to avoid deportation action.

Others exempt from deportation

Diplomats are, subject to some caveats, exempt from deportation under section 8(3) of the 1971 Act.

Commonwealth citizens and citizens of the Republic of Ireland, who were such citizens when the 1971 Act came into force on 1 January 1973, may be exempt from deportation. This exemption applies to both s3(5) and 3(6) deportations. In addition to being a citizen when the Act came into force, to be exempt, the individual must also have been ordinarily resident in the UK for five years immediately prior to the decision to deport, or immediately prior to their conviction. A person who has become ordinarily resident will not lose such status if they have remained here in breach of immigration laws (s7(2)). Understandably, and as is often the case when having to demonstrate continuous residence in immigration matters, time spent serving a custodial sentence or in immigration detention cannot be included in the relevant five-year period (s7(3)).

Windrush Scheme

In response to public outcry over the plight of Commonwealth citizens, principally from the West Indies, who faced removal and sometimes deportation despite having lived in the UK for many years, the government introduced the 'Windrush Scheme'. It's free to apply to this scheme, and if successful, British citizenship, a right of abode (a step short of full British citizenship, but it similarly means the individual is not subject to UK immigration control) or indefinite leave to remain will be granted. In addition to regularising status under Windrush, there is also a financial compensation scheme for those who have suffered detriment as a result of past Home Office treatment.

There are three ways of applying to the Windrush scheme, two of which require the client (or their parent) to be a citizen of a Commonwealth country.

1. **If the person came to the UK from a Commonwealth country, and they were settled in the UK before 1 January 1973**

If the individual has been living in the UK continuously or has the right of abode, they can apply for British citizenship, evidence they have the right of abode, or a document confirming that they hold indefinite leave to remain. As only British citizens are exempt from deportation, we recommend applying for British citizenship where possible. However, in order to receive British citizenship, the individual will be required to comply with the majority of the requirements contained at Section 6(1) or (2) of the British Nationality Act 1981. They are exempt from paying the naturalisation application fee, and they may also qualify for exemption from the knowledge of language and life in the UK requirement, if they were settled prior to 1 January 1973 or if they have the right of abode and have strong ties to the UK.

If they have left the UK for more than 2 years since 1973, they should still be able to apply for British citizenship, but only if they already hold indefinite leave to remain. If they were never granted indefinite leave to remain by the Secretary of State, you will need to consider whether they may be eligible to apply for indefinite leave to remain under the scheme now. Unfortunately, past criminality may result in the indefinite leave to remain application being refused; the Secretary of State will consider the individual's character, including whether their presence in the UK is conducive to the public good, before granting indefinite leave.

Many of those who may be eligible may have already been deported from the UK, so such individuals may be entitled to a returning resident visa, enabling them to return to the UK on an indefinite leave, or a 10 year multiple entry visit visa. Such eligibility will assist with a revocation application.

2. **Their parents came to the UK from a Commonwealth country before 1973**

If at least one of the client's parents is a Commonwealth citizen and was settled in the UK before 1 January 1973 or had a right to abode, the client may be eligible to apply to the Windrush Scheme if they were born in the UK, or came to live in the UK before reaching the age of 18. The client must have lived continuously in the UK since arriving or being born here to in order to register or naturalise as a British citizen under the BNA 1981. If they have not lived in the UK continuously, but are here lawfully, they may be eligible to apply for indefinite leave to remain. Again, character will be assessed.

3. **If the person came to the UK from any country before 31 December 1988**

A client may also be able to apply under the Windrush scheme if they can prove they came to live in the UK before 31 December 1988 and are now settled here. Such individuals do not need to be Commonwealth citizens; they can be of any nationality. The difficultly with these applications will be demonstrating that the person holds indefinite leave to remain, especially if such leave was issued in the 1980s. We have experience of a client who relocated to the UK before 1988, and it is believed that he secured indefinite leave to enter prior to his relocation, but he has no evidence to prove such status. His Home Office Subject Access Request also doesn't contain any information in relation to the leave granted in the 1980s.

As mentioned above, applications to the Windrush Scheme are free, so an application via this route should be a reasonably cheap, and straightforward, way of avoiding deportation proceedings in the event of a past conviction. Processing times are however long – cases can take many months to be decided.

CHAPTER THREE

FURTHER LEGISLATION – AUTOMATIC DEPORTATION

The public interest in deporting a foreign criminal remained, for many years, ultimately a matter of judicial discretion, paying due regard to the broadly-drafted provisions of the 1971 Act. Particularly after the Human Rights Act 1998 came into force, it was argued, often successfully, that deportation was a disproportionate breach of an individual's Article 8 right to respect for their private and family life.

Responding to numerous cases where it felt the balance had been incorrectly set, the government embarked on a series of changes to both primary legislation and Immigration Rules.

Perhaps the most significant changes to the UK's deportation landscape were introduced by the UK Borders Act 2007. What had for many years been discretionary powers became mandatory were effectively made mandatory under this legislation.

Under section 32 of the 2007 Act, a foreign criminal is defined as someone who is not British, who is convicted in the UK of an offence, and who is either sentenced to at least 12 months in prison, or whose offence was specified by order of the Secretary of State as particularly serious.

The Act, referring back to the 1971 legislation, also provides that the deportation of a "foreign criminal" under s32 "is conducive to the public good", and its *coup de grace* is contained in s32(4), under which "the Secretary of State **must** (our emphasis) make a deportation order in respect of a foreign criminal".

There are exceptions to this mandatory provision, the principal ones being:

- Certain Commonwealth and Irish citizens, as mentioned in Chapter 1
- Where removal from the UK would breach any person's rights under the Refugee Convention, European Convention on Human Rights, Convention Against Human Trafficking or the EU Treaties
- Where the Secretary of State 'thinks' the individual was under 18 at date of conviction

The nature of the power to deport contained in the 2007 Act shifted the starting point for a foreign criminal seeking to challenge a deportation decision. Persuading a tribunal judge that the automatic signing of an order was unlawful due to one of the above exceptions was evidentially far more difficult than challenging a s3(5) order. We always describe this to a client as, instead of starting at the foot of the mountain, they are now starting out from the bottom of the valley below. The climb is much longer, and much harder.

Note that, in relation to EU citizens, the 2007 Act has been amended to take account of Brexit; they will only be subject to these automatic deportation provisions for offences which consisted of or included conduct that took place after 31 December 2020. The deportation regime that applies to EU citizens and their family members is considered in detail in Chapter 6.

Not content with the way the courts interpreted these new provisions, the government again resorted to primary legislation; the Immigration Act 2014 was the vehicle for the introduction of a number of measures which sought to take yet more discretion away from the judiciary.

In an amendment to the Nationality, Immigration and Asylum Act 2002, the *public interest* was for the first time codified. A new Part 5A to the Act, in force from 28 July 2014, set out factors to be taken into account – and what weight was to be given to such factors – in primary legislation. So far as foreign criminals are concerned, the main provisions are contained in sections 117C-D. Echoing what s117C of the 2002 Act had to say about the "public good", the deportation of foreign criminals was, for the first time, stated to be "in the public interest"; the more serious the offence, the greater the public interest. Under s117C(3) the public interest "requires" deportation of someone convicted and sentenced to up to 4 years' imprisonment unless certain exceptions apply. These exceptions are, under s117C(4):

- The criminal has been lawfully resident in the UK for most of their life; and
- They are socially and culturally integrated in the UK; and
- There would be very significant obstacles to their integration into their own country

And under s117C(5):

- The criminal has a genuine and subsisting relationship with a qualifying partner, or a genuine and subsisting parental relationship with a qualifying child, and the effect of deportation on the partner or child would be unduly harsh

For criminals sentenced to 4 years or more, the bar was of course set even higher: under s117C(6) the public interest requires their deportation unless there are very compelling circumstances *over and above the exceptions summarised above.*

Section 117D is the interpretation section for the new Part 5A. It defines a "foreign criminal" as someone convicted of an offence and sentenced to at least 12 months' imprisonment, or convicted of an offence that "has caused serious harm", or is a "persistent offender". The provisions do not catch someone receiving consecutive sentences for various convictions which exceed 12 months but which, individually, do not.

It defines a "qualifying partner" as someone who is either British, or settled in the UK; a "qualifying child" is one who is under 18 and either British or who has lived in the UK continuously for 7 years or more. Who is a "partner" is not dictated by Appendix FM – see the Upper Tribunal decision in **Buci (Part 5A: "partner") [2020] UKUT 0008.**

At the same time as Part 5A entered into force, new Immigration Rules were introduced by House of Commons Paper HC532. The Supreme Court considered in **KO (Nigeria)** – discussed below – that it was "unnecessary to refer in detail to the Changes to the Immigration Rules made at the same time (paragraphs 398-399), since it is not argued that any differences are material to the issues before us. The prevailing view is that these rules, and the statute which they echo so closely, are intended to have the same effect. There are, however, certain differences which are worth bearing in mind.

Paragraph 398 conflates two overarching concepts in deportation, providing that the removal of someone who receives a sentence of at least 12 months is both *conducive to the public good* and *in the public interest.* It then provides a framework for considering the cases of criminals whose sentences were from 12 months up to 4 years; those whose offending was either persistent or caused serious harm; and those who were sentenced to 4 years or more.

Taking the most serious offenders first, that is the end of the story; the exceptions to deportation set out at paragraph 399 are simply unavailable to individuals sentenced to 4+ years; their deportation is both conducive and in the public interest, and can only be challenged on human rights or protection grounds.

For the others, paragraphs 399 and 399A contain a series of provisions that mirror those in section 117C of the 2002 Act. Thus deportation may be avoided if:

- The person has a genuine and subsisting parental relationship with a child under the age of 18 years who is in the UK; the child is a British Citizen; or has lived in the UK continuously for at least the 7 years immediately preceding the date of the immigration decision; and in either case it would be unduly harsh for the child to live in the country to which the person is to be deported; and it would be unduly harsh for the child to remain in the UK without the person who is to be deported; or

- The person has a genuine and subsisting relationship with a partner who is in the UK and is a British Citizen or settled in the UK; the relationship was formed at a time when the person was in the UK lawfully and their immigration status was not precarious; it would be unduly harsh for that partner to live in the country to which the person is to be deported, because of compelling circumstances over and above those described in paragraph EX.2. of Appendix FM (see below); and it would be unduly harsh for that partner to remain in the UK without the person who is to be deported; or

- The person has been lawfully resident in the UK for most of his life; he is socially and culturally integrated in the UK; and there would be very significant obstacles to his integration into the country to which it is proposed he is deported.

The cross-reference above in paragraph 399 to Appendix FM of the Immigration Rules is a point of interpretation. EX.2 states that "insurmountable obstacles" means the very significant difficulties which would be faced by the applicant or their partner in continuing their family life together outside the UK and which could not be overcome or would entail very serious hardship for the applicant or their partner.

If none of these factors avail your client, the public interest in their deportation will only be outweighed by other factors *where there are very compelling circumstances over and above those described in paragraphs 399 and 399A.*

CHAPTER FOUR

PRACTICAL CONSIDERATIONS

Taking instructions

Particularly where you client remains in detention, you will often receive initial contact from a family member of an individual who faces deportation action. You will be able to obtain outline details of the circumstances of your potential client's case, but there is of course no substitute for direct instructions from them.

Actually speaking with your client can be a challenge when they are serving a prison sentence. The situation alleviates somewhat if they have completed their criminal sentence and have been moved to the immigration detention estate, where basic mobile phones are issued, but such a move cannot be guaranteed. Often prisoners who have completed their sentence remain in prison, making the advisor's job significantly more difficult.

Remember that, in order to communicate with the Home Office or other sources on your client's behalf, a signed form of authority is required. Send this into the prison at the earliest opportunity, as it can take time to receive it back duly signed.

Lengthy calls with someone in prison are essentially impossible. Your client may be able to arrange for such a call (outside their standard call allowance) via the prison chaplaincy, their named officer or the foreign national offenders (FNO) officer who may be based at their particular institution.

Arranging a prison visit is the obvious answer to taking detailed instructions. In recent times in-person visits have been severely curtailed as a result of the Covid pandemic. Some prisons have been able to offer video calls but organising these has, in our experience, been very problematic, leading to delays in securing instructions. Faced with this situation, advisors should keep the Home Office updated, and seek an extension of time, for example where an initial response to a notice of intention to deport has been served. If you have an appeal deadline, it is not appropriate to request more time, or to lodge out of time with reasons. It is far preferable to lodge a protective, in-time appeal and seek detailed instructions from the client as soon as possible thereafter.

When things do get back to normal, distance often becomes a significant factor for the legal advisor. You may have been contacted by family who live close to your office, but the client may be incarcerated many miles away. Always consider if you are best-placed to accept instructions in such circumstances. In particular, is evidence from the family likely to be more important than the client's own account? In many cases, it is.

At Appendix A we have put together a list of suggested questions – or areas for questioning – that typically arise in deportation cases. Of course, as the judiciary regularly tells us, each case turns on its own facts, so these are by no means exhaustive.

It is important to remember, despite what your client may tell you, that a challenge to deportation is not an opportunity to re-hear their criminal case. Unless they have, through their criminal representatives, appealed against conviction or sentence, there is no mileage in putting forward arguments that the individual was wrongly-convicted in the first place. Many clients struggle to understand and accept this; firm advice is therefore required when their witness statement is being drafted.

Legal aid is not routinely available – or "in scope" – in standard "family-based" deportation cases and appeals, under the Legal Aid, Sentencing and Punishment of Offenders Act 2012. Only where a protection ground for resisting deportation is raised – be in on Refugee Convention or ECHR grounds – will legal aid generally be available. In other cases, it is nonetheless possible to secure free legal representation through the Legal Aid Agency's Exceptional Case Funding (ECF) process. Bear in mind that it can take several weeks to receive a decision on an ECF application – something to factor in when considering deadlines set by the Home Office.

All lawyers should remember and implement their duty to advise a client of their potential eligibility for free advice and representation, including ECF.

Initial advice

Once you have taken instructions, your client care, or engagement, letter should briefly recite the facts of the case, and outline the legal structures applicable to the decision (or potential decision, where none has yet been received but is reasonably anticipated). We recommend a fairly brief letter, to be sent by post (marked as Rule 39 correspondence if addressed to a prison) which importantly should also be shared with family members where they stand to be directly affected by any deportation action. These family members will often be your main source of instructions, and of evidence. They are, of course, best placed to dig out old letters, bank statements etc. to prove past residence in the UK. It is crucial the family is kept informed of the progress of the case, with your client's consent of course.

The timing of decisions to deport is unpredictable. They can come early in a criminal sentence, or right at the end. If approached by a foreign national offender sentenced to more than 12 months imprisonment (or a repeat offender with a lesser sentence) it is appropriate to accept instructions and begin work on that case immediately, rather than put things off until they hear from the Home Office. Sometimes no action is taken – again, this can be unpredictable. Usually it is. The best outcome you can achieve for a deportation client is a decision from the Secretary of State that, while your client's offending is considered serious, on this occasion deportation action is not being pursued. This should of course put your client on notice that any further offending is likely to be dimly viewed.

Witness statements

These form a central part of the evidence in any deportation case. Obtaining a final, agreed version from a client in prison can be time-consuming, so factor this into your case preparation. Some prisoners, and certainly those in immigration detention, can access email, which speeds things up considerably. If not, sending draft statements back and forth between your office and prison can take weeks, especially if your client has a long and complex story to tell.

Securing statements from other witnesses is your next priority. Practically these will often be easier to take. Always remember to request proof of a deponent's identity – a scan of their current passport photo page or driving licence is preferred – to be annexed to their statement.

If there are children directly affected by your client's proposed deportation, consider whether they are old enough to give evidence. Younger children can be asked to write, in their own words, how they would feel if their family member had to leave the country without then, but sensitivity is key.

It is one thing for a younger child to write a letter; quite another for them to be asked to attend and give oral evidence at an appeal hearing. Other than its general case management powers set out in its general practice direction, the Immigration and Asylum Chamber (IAC) of the Tribunal has no specific rules on hearing from children, but an advisor must bear in mind the potential stress that answering questions before a judge might place on a young person.

External evidence

This can often make or break your client's case, especially where they must prove past residence in the UK. The Court of Appeal said in **AA (Nigeria) v SSHD [2020] EWCA Civ 1296** at para 13:

> *every foreign criminal who appeals against a deportation order by reference to his human rights must negotiate a formidable hurdle before his appeal will succeed... He needs to be in a position to assemble and present powerful evidence.*

While cautioning against a prescriptive approach, Popplewell LJ goes on to usefully summarise the following key areas of evidence-gathering:

> (a) the depth of the claimant's integration in United Kingdom society in terms of family, employment and otherwise;
>
> (b) the quality of his relationship with any child, partner or other family member in the United Kingdom;
>
> (c) the extent to which any relationship with family members might reasonably be sustained even after deportation, whether by their joining him abroad or otherwise;
>
> (d) the impact of his deportation on the need to safeguard and promote the welfare of any child in the United Kingdom;

(e) the likely strength of the obstacles to his integration in the society of the country of his nationality; and, surely in every case;

(f) any significant risk of his reoffending in the United Kingdom, judged, no doubt with difficulty, in the light of his criminal record set against the credibility of his probable assertions of remorse and reform.

In Appendix B we provide a non-exhaustive list of potential evidence you might consider obtaining on your client's behalf. Particularly in EEA deportations, providing past residence in the UK for a 5 or 10-year period prior to conviction for the index offence (the one that led to deportation action commencing) will be vital. In non-EEA deports, it will be evidence of family ties that has the best potential to challenge the decision.

It is best practice in every case to obtain disclosure of your client's Home Office records via a subject access request under the Data Protection Act 2018. You should make, as early as possible, a similar application to the Ministry of Justice in relation to prison records; this can be made via email quoting full personal details including prisoner number and enclosing client's authority to data.access@hmps.gsi.gov.uk or by post to:

HM Prison and Probation Service
Branston Registry
Building 16, S & T Store
Burton Road
Branston
Burton-on-Trent
Staffordshire
DE14 3EG

Prison records can reveal a wealth of useful information; for example, visiting records to show that your client has seen their partner and children regularly, or has called home frequently. If they have gained trusted prisoner status, and conducted themselves in a positive manner during service of their sentence, that will also weigh in their favour, albeit to a relatively small extent. Importantly, a prisoner's records should contain pre-sentence and OASys reports, which can contain a wealth of information about their particular characteristics, and the precise nature of their offending. These reports, having been prepared by Probation

Service professionals in accordance with a clear framework of factors, are favoured by tribunal judges in particular when such cases come before them.

Less usefully, you may also uncover evidence of adjudications for bad behaviour or breaches of prison rules. You are under no duty to disclose this to the Home Office, who will of course be able to find it if they look for it in any event. Tactically, however, it is usually best to adopt a policy of full disclosure so that a Home Office Presenting Officer cannot spring a surprise at a hearing with evidence that reflects badly on your client.

Expert evidence

Obtaining the opinion of an expert can be central to a deportation case, and particularly an appeal. In family-based cases, where removal is resisted with reference to Article 8 ECHR, such evidence will typically come from an independent social worker or psychologist. The former will assess the family situation and the potential impact on partner and children of an individual's deportation. The latter will consider similar matters, but importantly can also assess propensity of an individual to re-offend. They are significantly more expensive to instruct than social workers, in our experience.

Bear in mind, once again, the practicalities of using an expert. Do they need to meet the client in-person or via a video call? How will this be arranged, and in what timescale is it possible? Advisors are often – rightly in our view – reluctant to expend the client's funds on an expert pre-decision. However, leaving instruction until after an appeal has been lodged can lead to problems with timing. If expert evidence is crucial to your appeal, apply for an adjournment with detailed reasons and a timetable for obtaining the report.

We consider this, and other aspects of appeals management, in Chapter 6.

Drafting representations

Often, you will be approached by, or on behalf of, a client who has received a notice from the Home Office that deportation action is being considered against them. These notices invite a response, setting out reasons why the client believes they should not be deported.

The best way to present such arguments on your client's behalf is in the form of detailed written representations, supported by witness and other evidence. Late instructions may mean it is impossible to achieve a fully-evidenced response; in that case, a written submission, based on initial instructions, and promising evidence in support, should be sent. The gap between the first Home Office letter intimating an intention to deport and the actual notice of decision can be many months.

When drafting representations, as well as setting out arguments as to why a deportation order should not be issued, together with assertions in relation to why the individual is likely to face a real risk of serious irreversible harm if removed before the appeals process has been finalised. The possibility of such early removal – under section 94B NIAA 2002 – is a significant prospect in deportation cases, and must be anticipated.

Detention and bail

Once your client has completed their criminal sentence, they should automatically be considered for a grant of immigration bail by the Home Office. This does not always happen, however, so advisors should be aware of the estimated date of release (EDR) in order to prepare for the client's release.

Written representations should first be made directly to the Secretary of State; typically these are addressed to the Criminal Casework Directorate, although terminology within UK Visas and Immigration is liable to change at short notice. If release is not sanctioned, an application for bail may be made to the First tier Tribunal.

We do not cover the law on detention and bail in detail in this book, but a useful and detailed source for law and practice is the Guidance on Immigration Bail for Judges of the First-tier Tribunal (Immigration and Asylum Chamber), issued on 15 January 2018.

CHAPTER FIVE

KEY LEGAL CONCEPTS

As a result of the piecemeal amendment to legislation and immigration rules set out in preceding chapters, advisors are faced with a rather confusing – often overlapping – mix of concepts, some or all of which will be relevant to your client's case. In this chapter we consider how the Home Office, and most importantly the judiciary, have interpreted these words and phrases.

A complete code

The idea that the combined force of legislation and rules constitutes a "complete code" in family-type (as opposed to protection-type) deportation cases – unlike in any other area of immigration law – has dogged those facing deportation in recent years. In **NE-A (Nigeria) v Secretary of State for the Home Department** [2017] **EWCA Civ 239** the Court of Appeal confirmed that the obligation to "have regard to" sections 117B and (where applicable) section 117C meant that the statutory scheme constitutes a "complete code" for the consideration of Article 8 ECHR in the context of deportation.

The stated view of Parliament is that the purpose of the statutory scheme is to require decision-makers to adopt a structured approach to the Article 8 issues raised by the removal of a foreign national. That is, whether removal will constitute a disproportionate interference with, and thus a breach of, Article 8 rights, and whether the 'complete code' ensures that due weight is given to the public interest. It is no part of its purpose to prevent the proper application of Article 8. This is clearly stated in para. 26 of the judgment in **NA (Pakistan) v SSHD** [2016] **EWCA Civ 662**. Following from that, the statutory structure is a "complete code" in the sense that the entirety of the proportionality assessment required by Article 8 can and must be conducted within it.

It follows that the Strasbourg case-law about the application of Article 8 in cases of this kind must and can be accommodated within the statutory structure. Important guidance about removals generally is given in **Jeunesse (12738/10)**, and there are three well-known cases concerning foreign criminals – **Boultif v Switzerland (2001) 33 EHRR 50, Üner v Netherlands (2007) 45 EHRR 14,** and **Maslov v Austria** [2009] **INLR** 47. At para. 38 of its judgment in **NA (Pakistan)** the Court said:

> *[T]he Secretary of State and the tribunals and courts will have regard to the Strasbourg jurisprudence when applying the tests set out in our domestic legislation. For example, a tribunal may be considering whether it would be 'unduly harsh' for a child to remain in England without the deportee; or it may be considering whether certain circumstances are sufficiently 'compelling' to outweigh the high public interest in deportation of foreign criminals. Anyone applying these tests (as required by our own rules and legislation) should heed the guidance contained in the Strasbourg authorities. As we have stated above, the scheme of Part 5A of the 2002 Act and paras. 398-399A of the 2014 rules is to ensure compliance with the requirements of Article 8 through a structured approach, which is intended to ensure that proper weight is given to the public interest in deportation whilst also having regard to other relevant factors as identified in the Strasbourg and domestic caselaw. The new regime is not intended to produce violations of Article 8.*

The Court goes on at para 39 to make the point that "assessments under Article 8 may not lead to identical results in every ECHR contracting state", reflecting the margin of appreciation which the Convention allows in their assessment of the public interest.

Unduly Harsh

It will often be necessary to argue on behalf of your client that the effect of deportation on their children would be "unduly harsh", within the meaning of section 117C(5) – i.e. Exception 2 – and paragraph 399(a) of the Rules. The courts have considered on many occasions the height of the threshold which that phrase sets.

Guidance as to the meaning of 'unduly harsh' in this context was given by the Upper Tribunal (McCloskey J President and UT Judge Perkins) in **MK (Sierra Leone) v Secretary of State for the Home Department [2015] UKUT 223 (IAC)**, para 46. They referred to the 'evaluative assessment' required of the tribunal:

> *By way of self-direction, we are mindful that "unduly harsh" does not equate with uncomfortable, inconvenient, undesirable or merely difficult. Rather, it poses a considerably more elevated threshold. "Harsh" in this context denotes something severe, or bleak. It is the antithesis of pleasant or comfortable. Furthermore, the addition of the adverb "unduly" raises an already elevated standard still higher.'"*

Currently the judicial high-water mark is the Supreme Court decision in **KO (Nigeria) and others v SSHD [2018] UKSC 53.**

The only judgment, with which the other members of the Court agreed, was given by Lord Carnwath. He quoted from **MK (Sierra Leone)**, describing the tribunal's guidance as "authoritative". In his view, the expression 'unduly harsh' seems clearly intended to introduce a higher hurdle than that of 'reasonableness' under section 117B(6), taking account of the public interest in the deportation of foreign criminals. Further the word 'unduly' implies an element of comparison. It assumes that there is a 'due' level of 'harshness', that is a level which may be acceptable or justifiable in the relevant context. 'Unduly' implies something going beyond that level.

The relevant context is that set by section 117C(1), that is the public interest in the deportation of foreign criminals. One is looking for a degree of harshness going beyond what would necessarily be involved for any child faced with the deportation of a parent. What it does not require in is a balancing of relative levels of severity of the parent's offence, other than is inherent in the distinction drawn by the section itself by reference to length of sentence. Nor (contrary to the view of the Court of Appeal in **IT (Jamaica) v Secretary of State for the Home Department [2016] EWCA Civ 932**, paras 55, 64) can it be equated with a requirement to show 'very compelling reasons'. That would be in effect to replicate the additional test applied by section 117C(6) with respect to sentences of four years or more.

In order to establish that the word "unduly" was not directed to the relative seriousness issue it was necessary for Lord Carnwath to say to what it was in fact directed. The effect of what he says is that "unduly" is directed to the degree of harshness required: some level of harshness is to be regarded as "acceptable or justifiable" in the context of the public interest in the deportation of foreign criminals, and what "unduly" does is to provide that Exception 2 will only apply where the harshness goes beyond that level. Lord Carnwath's focus is not primarily on how to define the "acceptable" level of harshness. It is true that he refers to a degree of harshness "going beyond what would necessarily be involved for any child faced with the deportation of a parent", but that cannot be read entirely literally: it is hard to see how one would define the level of harshness that would "necessarily" be suffered by "any" child (indeed one can imagine unusual cases where the deportation of a parent would not be "harsh" for the child at all, even where there was a genuine and subsisting relationship). The underlying concept is clearly of an enhanced degree of harshness sufficient to outweigh the public interest in the deportation of foreign criminals in the medium offender category.

Lord Carnwath goes on to note that **MK (Sierra Leone)** was followed in the later case of **MAB (USA) v Secretary of State for the Home Department** [**2015**] **UKUT 435**. On the facts of **MK**, the Upper Tribunal held that the test was satisfied:

> *Approached in this way, we have no hesitation in concluding that it would be unduly harsh for either of the two seven year old British citizen children concerned to be abruptly uprooted from their United Kingdom life setting and lifestyle and exiled to this struggling, impoverished and plague stricken West African state. No reasonable or right thinking person would consider this anything less than cruel.'*

The tribunal in **MK** considered both the scenario where the appellant's children accompanied him to Sierra Leone, and the scenario where they stayed in the UK. The passage quoted by Lord Carnwath refers to the former scenario, and the tribunal's conclusion about it was obviously right. Lord Carnwath does not quote the tribunal's conclusion on the latter scenario, which it also found to be unduly harsh.

The essential point is that the criterion of undue harshness sets a bar which is "elevated" and carries a "much stronger emphasis" than mere undesirability. The tribunal's self-direction uses a battery of synonyms and antonyms: although these should not be allowed to become a substitute for the statutory language, tribunals may find them of some assistance as a reminder of the elevated nature of the test. The reason why some degree of harshness is acceptable is that there is a strong public interest in the deportation of foreign criminals (including medium offenders). The underlying question for tribunals is whether the harshness which the deportation will cause for the partner and/or child is of a sufficiently elevated degree to outweigh that public interest.

However, while recognising the "elevated" nature of the statutory test, it is important not to lose sight of the fact that the hurdle which it sets is not as high as that set by the test of "very compelling circumstances" in section 117C(6). As Lord Carnwath points out in the second part of para. 23 of his judgment, disapproving **IT (Jamaica)**, if that were so the position of medium offenders and their families would be no better than that of serious offenders. It follows that the observations in the case-law to the effect that it will be rare for the test of "very compelling circumstances" to be satisfied have no application in this context. The statutory intention is evidently that the hurdle representing the unacceptable impact on a partner or child should be set somewhere between the (low) level applying in the case of persons who are liable to ordinary immigration removal and the (very high) level applying to serious offenders.

Observations of that kind are helpful, but they cannot identify an objectively measurable standard. It is inherent in the nature of an exercise of the kind required by section 117C(5) that Parliament intended that tribunals should in each case make an informed evaluative assessment of whether the effect of the deportation of the parent or partner on their child or partner would be "unduly harsh" in the context of the strong public interest in the deportation of foreign criminals; and further exposition of that phrase will never be of more than limited value.

The test under section 117C(5) does indeed require an appellant to establish a degree of harshness going beyond a threshold "acceptable" level. It is not necessarily wrong to describe that as an "ordinary" level of harshness. However, the phrase may be misleading if used incautiously. The courts have noted two (related) risks. First, "ordinary" is capable of being understood as meaning anything which is not exceptional, or in any event rare. That is not the correct approach. There is no reason in principle why cases of "undue" harshness may not occur quite commonly. Secondly, if tribunals treat the essential question as being "is this level of harshness out of the ordinary?" they may be tempted to find that Exception 2 does not apply simply on the basis that the situation fits into some commonly-encountered pattern. That would be dangerous.

How a child will be affected by a parent's deportation will depend on an almost infinitely variable range of circumstances and it is not possible to identify a baseline of "ordinariness". Simply by way of example, the degree of harshness of the impact may be affected by the child's age; by whether the parent lives with them; by the degree of the child's emotional dependence on the parent; by the financial consequences of his deportation; by the availability of emotional and financial support from a remaining parent and other family members; by the practicability of maintaining a relationship with the deported parent; and of course by all the individual characteristics of the child.

Unlike the bold approach taken in **KO (Nigeria)**, the Court of Appeal has in recent years been conservative in its approach to deportation principles. However, taking its lead from the Supreme Court, it has in late 2020 issued several judgments which adopt a more purposive, robust approach to the impact of deportation on children, and on the unduly harsh test in particular, starting with its judgment in **HA (Iraq) v Secretary of State for the Home Department** [2020] **EWCA Civ 117**.

In **HA (Iraq)** the court effectively sealed the restoration of a flexible, child-centred approach to the unduly harsh test. The case began life in the Tribunal system as **RA (s117C "unduly harsh2; offence; seriousness) Iraq [2019] UKUT 00123 (IAC)**. Two Iraqi citizens with British children received sentences of 16 months (HA, for immigration offences) and 12 months (RA, for an identity document offence). Both appellants had won in the First-tier Tribunal, but those decisions were successfully appealed by the Secretary of State and were dismissed substantively by the Upper Tribunal.

The court (Underhill LJ) examined in detail what exactly Lord Carnwath was saying – and what he was not saying – in paragraph 23 of **KO (Nigeria)**. The search for a "degree of harshness going beyond what would necessarily be involved for any child faced with the deportation of a parent" was not to be taken literally.

Paragraph 15 of **HA (Iraq)** refers back to **KO (Nigeria)** and sets out a helpful summary of the unduly harsh test:

> *(1) The unduly harsh test is to be determined without reference to the criminality of the parent or the severity of the relevant offences:* ***KO (Nigeria)*** *para 23, reversing in this respect the Court of Appeal's decision in that case, reported under the name* ***MM (Uganda) v Secretary of State for the Home Department [2016] EWCA Civ 617****, in which at paragraph 26 Laws LJ expressed this court's conclusion that the unduly harsh test required regard to be had to all the circumstances including the criminal's immigration and criminal history.*
>
> *(2) "Unduly" harsh requires a degree of harshness which goes beyond what would necessarily be involved for any child faced with deportation of a parent:* ***KO (Nigeria)*** *para 23.*
>
> *(3) That is an elevated test, which carries a much stronger emphasis that mere undesirability or what is merely uncomfortable, inconvenient, or difficult; but the threshold is not as high as the very compelling circumstances test in s. 117C(6):* ***KO (Nigeria)*** *para 27;* ***HA (Iraq)*** *paras 51-52.*
>
> *(4) The formulation in para 23 of* ***KO (Nigeria)*** *does not posit some objectively measurable standard of harshness which is acceptable, and it is potentially misleading and dangerous to seek to identify some "ordinary" level of harshness as an acceptable level by reference to what may be commonly encountered circumstances: there is no reason in principle why cases of undue hardship may not occur quite commonly;*

and how a child will be affected by a parent's deportation will depend upon an almost infinitely variable range of circumstances; it is not possible to identify a base level of "ordinariness": ***HA (Iraq)*** *paras 44, 50-53, 56 and 157,* ***AA (Nigeria) v Secretary of State for the Home Department [2020] EWCA Civ 1296*** *at para 12.*

(5) Beyond this guidance, further exposition of the phrase will rarely be helpful; and tribunals will not err in law if they carefully evaluate the effect of the parent's deportation on the particular child and then decide whether the effect is not merely harsh but unduly harsh applying the above guidance: ***HA (Iraq)*** *at paras 53 and 57. There is no substitute for the statutory wording.*

The impact of – and on – children

As we have seen when discussing the "unduly harsh" test, many clients seeking to challenge deportation rely on relationships they have with qualifying children. On 2 November 2009, section 55 of the Borders, Citizenship and Immigration Act 2009 (BCIA 2009) came into force. Section 55 requires the Secretary of State to have regard to the need to safeguard and promote the welfare of children in the UK. The Act applies to children generally, not just those who are British or who have lived in the UK for a specific period of time. It requires Home Office decision makers to be vigilant when considering cases involving children, and to ensure that any children affected by the decision will not be at risk of harm.

In the immigration world, s55 has been the subject of extensive judicial interpretation. The leading judgment on s55 is the Supreme Court decision in **ZH (Tanzania) v SSHD [2011] UKSC 4.** The case concerns the Tanzanian mother of two British children who were aged 12 and 9 at the time of the judgment. The children were both born in the UK and acquired British citizen at birth from their British father. The parents had subsequently separated and were not in a relationship at the time of the decision. Although the children continued to spend time with their father, they resided with their mother on a permanent basis.

ZH had a poor immigration history. She arrived in the UK in 1995 at the age of 20, and had made three unsuccessful claims for asylum, one using her true identity and two using false ones. She subsequently submitted four applications seeking leave to remain with reference to the ECHR or Home Office policies. Her most recent application was submitted in 2007, after the children's father had been diagnosed with HIV. The Secretary of State refused this application, but concluded that the application created a realistic prospect of success, enabling ZH to pursue an appeal before the First-tier Tribunal.

The tribunal dismissed the appeal, but the case was soon before the Upper Tribunal. In addition to finding that the Appellant was not credible, the Upper Tribunal found it a "distinct and very real possibility" that the children might remain in the UK with their father, and also that it would be "a very valid decision" for the children to return to Tanzania with their mother. The case subsequently came before the Court of Appeal and Supreme Court.

The Supreme Court considers the relevance of s55 in an immigration context. When considering the weight to be afforded to such a protection, the court references Article 3(1) of the UNCRC, which states as follows:

> *"In all actions concerning children, whether undertaken by public of private social welfare institutions, courts of law, administrative authorities or legislative bodies, the best interests of the child shall be a primary consideration."* [our emphasis]

Lady Hale subsequently acknowledges that, *""a primary consideration" is not the same as* ***the*** *primary consideration"*', and that a primary consideration is less than '*"the paramount consideration"*'. Lord Kerr adds that, as a primary consideration, the best interests of the child *"... is a factor... that must rank higher than any other... Where the best interests of the child clearly favour a certain course, that course should be followed unless countervailing reasons of considerable force displace them."*

When considering the best interests of the child, a balancing exercising is necessary; when asserting that removal is not proportionate under Article 8(2), one must ask whether it would be reasonable to expect a child to live in another country, and why such a course of action would not be reasonable. Whilst British nationality is not a trump card, the Supreme Court acknowledges that *"it is of particular importance in assessing the best interests of any child."* The court further held that various factors will be relevant to such a consideration, including the child's UK integration; length of absence from the other country; where and with whom the child will live with; arrangements for care in the other country; strength of the children's relationships with their parents and other family members in the UK.

Despite the Appellant's poor immigration history, the Supreme Court reached a unanimous decision to allow the appeal. The findings in the case are extremely helpful, and the following are important conclusions which may be incorporated into deportation representations and skeleton arguments:

At paragraph 32 Lady Hale concludes as follows:

> *32. Nor should the intrinsic importance of citizenship be played down. As citizens these children have rights which they will not be able to exercise if they move to another country. They will lose the advantages of growing up and being educated in their own country, their own culture and their own language. They will have lost all this when they come back as adults.*

Lady Hale confirms further guidance in relation to the application of s55:

> *33. We now have a much greater understanding of the importance of these issues in assessing the overall well-being of the child. In making the proportionality assessment under article 8, the best interests of the child must be a primary consideration. This means that they must be considered first. They can, of course, be outweighed by the cumulative effect of other considerations. In this case, the countervailing considerations were the need to maintain firm and fair immigration control, coupled with the mother's appalling immigration history and the precariousness of her position when family life was created. But, as the Tribunal rightly pointed out, the children were not to be blamed for that. And the inevitable result of removing their primary carer would be that they had to leave with her.*

At paragraph 46 Lord Kerr notes:

> *46. It is a universal theme of the various international and domestic instruments to which Lady Hale has referred that, in reaching decisions that will affect a child, a primacy of importance must be accorded to his or her best interests. This is not, it is agreed, a factor of limitless importance in the sense that it will prevail over all other considerations. It is a factor, however, that must rank higher than any other. It is not merely one consideration that weighs in the balance alongside other competing factors. Where the best interests of the child clearly favour a certain course, that course should be followed unless countervailing reasons of considerable force displace them. It is not necessary to express this in terms of a presumption but the primacy of this consideration needs to be made clear in emphatic terms. What is determined to be in a child's best interests should customarily dictate the outcome of cases such as the present, therefore, and it will require considerations of substantial moment to permit a different result.*

The effect of s55 came before the Supreme Court again in the case of **Zoumbas v SSHD [2013] UKSC 74.** At paragraph 10 of his judgment, Lord Hodge, delivering the judgment of the court, summarised the seven legal principles relevant to cases involving an assessment of s55:

> *(1) The best interests of a child are an integral part of the proportionality assessment under article 8 ECHR;*
>
> *(2) In making that assessment, the best interests of a child must be a primary consideration, although not always the only primary consideration; and the child's best interests do not of themselves have the status of the paramount consideration;*
>
> *(3) Although the best interests of a child can be outweighed by the cumulative effect of other considerations, no other consideration can be treated as inherently more significant;*
>
> *(4) While different judges might approach the question of the best interests of a child in different ways, it is important to ask oneself the right questions in an orderly manner in order to avoid the risk that the*

> *best interests of a child might be undervalued when other important considerations were in play;*
>
> *(5) It is important to have a clear idea of a child's circumstances and of what is in a child's best interests before one asks oneself whether those interests are outweighed by the force of other considerations;*
>
> *(6) To that end there is no substitute for a careful examination of all relevant factors when the interests of a child are involved in an article 8 assessment; and*
>
> *(7) A child must not be blamed for matters for which he or she is not responsible, such as the conduct of a parent.*

In **EV (Philippines) and others v SSHD** [2014] **EWCA Civ 874**, the Court of Appeal accepted that *"The best interests of the child are to be determined by reference to the child alone without reference to the immigration history or status of either parent".* At paragraph 35, the Court further clarified the factors to be taken into account when considering the best interest of a child:

> *35. A decision as to what is in the best interests of children will depend on a number of factors such as (a) their age; (b) the length of time that they have been here; (c) how long they have been in education; (c) what stage their education has reached; (d) to what extent they have become distanced from the country to which it is proposed that they return; (e) how renewable their connection with it may be; (f) to what extent they will have linguistic, medical or other difficulties in adapting to life in that country; and (g) the extent to which the course proposed will interfere with their family life or their rights (if they have any) as British citizens.*

Whereas section 117C(5) refers simply to "the effect of C's deportation on the partner or child [being] unduly harsh", the equivalent provisions of paragraph 399 (that is, points (a) and (b) under the parent case and points (ii) and (iii) under the partner case) identify two distinct scenarios – the scenario where the child/partner would go with the deportee ("the go scenario") and the scenario where they would stay behind without him ("the stay scenario").

Modern Means of Communication

Intrinsically tied up in consideration of the impact of deportation on children, this phrase has gained popularity – or more accurately notoriety – in Home Office refusal decisions. The authors had discussed leaving it out of this book, as the wording seemed to have fallen out of use, but several recent deportation decisions we have seen again cite it as a reasonable alternative to allowing a foreign national criminal to remain in the UK.

From around 2010, modern means of communication becomes a glib copy-and-paste feature of many Home Office refusals; a regular feature in case law. An early example is the High Court decision in **ZA (Nigeria) v SSHD [2010] EWHC 718 (Admin)**. A January 2010 decision letter is quoted, containing the phrase. Foskett J concluded the decision was legitimately made, having regard to the Applicant's ability to return home and apply for entry clearance.

But the phrase holds greater significance in the deportation context, when speedy return following removal is far from certain. By strange coincidence, on the same day as deciding **ZA (Nigeria)**, Foskett J heard another judicial review challenge, of a refusal to revoke a deportation order in respect of the applicant in **R (Stephenson) v SSHD [2010] EWHC 704 (Admin)**. It was more specifically a challenge to the certification of a human rights claim under section 94 of the 2002 Act. The phrase appears in the Secretary of State's decision letter of June 2009; a decision that was quashed by the court, without explicit consideration of how a family might stay together while separated by several thousand miles. Focus here was on their ability to live as a single unit outside the UK, with the judge anticipating amendments to the 2002 Act by the Immigration Act 2014. In considering the difference between removal and deportation, he said:

> *"...the difference in aim is potentially important because the factors in favour of expulsion are in my view capable of carrying greater weight in a deportation case than in a case of ordinary removal... I think it perfectly possible in principle for a given set of considerations of family life and/or private life to be sufficiently weighty to render expulsion*

> *disproportionate in an ordinary removal case, yet insufficient to render expulsion disproportionate in a deportation case because of the additional weight to be given to the criminal offending on which the deportation decision was based."*

This approach, codified in Part 5A of the 2002 Act and endlessly considered in reported Tribunal decisions since it was introduced, brought the significance of modern communications to the fore in the minds of officials and the judiciary. Just a month later, in **SS (India) v SSHD [2010] EWCA Civ 388**, the Court of Appeal was less than complimentary about the phrase, in examining the Secretary of State's and Tribunal's reliance on modern communications such as "the telephone, internet and texting"; the court stated in the context of a proposed deportation:

> *"The AIT concluded somewhat lamely at paragraph 40 that there could be some degree of family life through "modern means of communication" and possible visits to India. But that conclusion sits ill with the earlier finding, in paragraph 38, that Navdeep and Pardeep are extremely close to their father and seek his guidance in all the big decisions in their life."*

Blake J was similarly disdainful in the statutory appeal of **Omotunde (best interests – Zambrano applied – Razgar) Nigeria [2011] UKUT 00247(IAC):**

> *"We conclude that deportation of the father to Nigeria would deprive Tolu of his dominant carer throughout his young life, and seriously interrupt his daily care arrangements. We reject the submission that family life hitherto enjoyed between an active parent and a small child could be appropriately maintained by telephone calls or other 'modern methods of communication' from Nigeria. We note that this Tribunal reached a similar conclusion in LD (Article 8- best interest of child) Zimbabwe [2010] UKUT 278 (IAC). Difficult as the issues in a case such as the present are to decide, their resolution is not assisted by wholly unrealistic suggestions such as this."*

It has sometimes been argued that the particular characteristics of a family member – a disability such as autism for example – makes electronic or remote communication impossible. In **AR (Pakistan) v SSHD [2010] EWCA Civ 816** for example, counsel made this argument in respect of a disabled child. His argument was rejected:

> *"It was accepted by all concerned that the children could not move to Pakistan and that if the appellant were deported his son could not maintain effective contact with him, as might have been possible but for his disability. The panel also took into account the particular nature and degree of that disability and the extent to which the appellant had been in contact with his children and had provided parental support. In my view there are no grounds for holding that the panel erred in law by adopting the wrong approach [in dismissing AR's appeal]."*

In the past decade, cases have tended to treat this phrase rather perfunctorily. See, for example, the Upper Tribunal's decision in Jarusevicius (EEA Reg 21 – effect of imprisonment) [2012] UKUT 00120(IAC), where it concluded that the lower court had not sought to minimise the impact of separation on the child of a deported parent in referencing modern means of communication:

> *"It would be an error of approach if they had, but in context, we conclude that it was merely observing that removal need not necessarily lead to a total and permanent rupture."*

While judges generally agree that maintaining a relationship at distance isn't good for a child, it remains just one factor in consideration of the public interest in deportation of a parent. To ensure the Secretary of State and the courts look at this issue with sufficient care, evidence of the impact of separation is of course crucial.

Very Significant Obstacles to Integration

Under s117C(4) of the NIAA 2002 – "Exception 1" – deportation may be resisted by an individual who has been lawfully resident in the UK for most of his life, is socially and culturally integrated in the UK, and where "there would be very significant obstacles to his integration in the country to where he is to be deported." For clients long-resident in the UK the first two parts of the test will be satisfied; it is the last part, regarding obstacles to integration abroad, on which the outcome of a case will usually turn.

In **Kamara v SSHD [2016] EWCA Civ** Sales LJ, as he then was, considered that a broad, evaluative judgement had to be made:

> *In my view, the concept of a foreign criminal's "integration" into the country to which it is proposed that he be deported, as set out in section 117C(4)(c) and paragraph 399A, is a broad one. It is not confined to the mere ability to find a job or to sustain life while living in the other country. It is not appropriate to treat the statutory language as subject to some gloss and it will usually be sufficient for a court or tribunal simply to direct itself in the terms that Parliament has chosen to use. The idea of "integration" calls for a broad evaluative judgment to be made as to whether the individual will be enough of an insider in terms of understanding how life in the society in that other country is carried on and a capacity to participate in it, so as to have a reasonable opportunity to be accepted there, to be able to operate on a day-to-day basis in that society and to build up within a reasonable time a variety of human relationships to give substance to the individual's private or family life."*

Remember that deportation is not just removal – it is described in some cases as "exile". See for example **Lowe v SSHD [2021] EWCA Civ 62**, where the appellant was a young Jamaican man still largely dependent on his UK-resident parents. The fact that he had not lived independently of his parents was a factor in the First tier Tribunal concluding that very significant obstacles to his removal existed. The Upper Tribunal reversed that decision, but was itself overturned by the Court of Appeal, having regard to "*this* young man, with all his characteristics, attributes, qualities and defects that were disclosed in evidence". The decision of the FTT could in no way be described as irrational.

Very Compelling Circumstances

For criminals sentenced to 4 years imprisonment or more, their deportation is required, in the public interest, unless "very compelling circumstances" can be shown, over and above the matters set out in "Exceptions" listed at ss117C(4) & (5) of the NIAA 2002.

Two difficulties about the construction of section 117C(6) were resolved by the Court of Appeal in **NA (Pakistan) v Secretary of State for the Home Department** [2016] **EWCA Civ 662.**

First, on a literal reading sub-section (6) applies only to serious offenders and not to medium offenders, with the result that in such a case, if neither of the Exceptions applies, deportation must be treated as justified whatever "very compelling circumstances" there might be. However, the Court held that such a reading would be neither rational nor consistent with the ECHR and cannot have been what Parliament intended; it would also be inconsistent with paragraph 398 of the Immigration Rules. The court held that it was necessary to read sub-section (6) as applying equally in the case of medium offenders governed by sub-section (3): see paras. 25-27 of its judgment given by Jackson LJ. The need for that correction was not controversial, and indeed the Secretary of State positively invited the Court to hold as it did.

Secondly, the phrase in section 117C(6) "very compelling circumstances, over and above those described in Exceptions 1 and 2" might be read as excluding circumstances which fell within the scope of those Exceptions, so that (for example) potential deportees could not rely on the effect of their deportation on a qualifying child, even if it would otherwise be material to the assessment of whether there were very compelling circumstances outweighing the public interest in deportation. The Court held that that was not what was meant.

The assessment of "very compelling circumstances" will, of course, be fact-sensitive. The case of **SSHD v Starkey** [2021] **EWCA Civ 421** illustrates this, with successive tribunals taking a different view on the evidence before them. S was a citizen of South Africa, convicted and sentenced to 8 years' imprisonment. He appealed the decision to deport him, arguing that, whilst there was the public interest in his deportation, there were very compelling circumstances that outweighed that interest, namely his mental health condition and the lack of support that he would obtain in South Africa, and that therefore NIAA 2002 s 117C(6) had applied. The First tier Tribunal found there was no satisfactory evidence to suggest that S would not receive the immediate treatment he required in South Africa, and that his mental health would not impede his integration there. The Upper Tribunal disagreed, taking the view that the evidence did lead to a conclusion that S would face inhuman or degrading treatment contrary to Article 3 ECHR if returned home. The Court of Appeal disagreed once again, finding the Upper Tribunal had misunderstood the evidence about the severity of S's illness.

Length of sentence

This is a relevant consideration, most notably in cases where an individual is sentenced to between 12 months and 4 years. In principle a potential deportee can therefore rely, as part of the overall proportionality assessment, on the fact that his offence was at or near the bottom of the scale of seriousness. That conclusion is also in accordance with the Strasbourg jurisprudence, to which, as is confirmed both by **NA (Pakistan)** and by **Hesham Ali**, courts are obliged to have regard. In **Boultif** the European Court of Human Rights held in terms that it was necessary in the assessment of the proportionality of deportation to take into account "the nature and seriousness of the offence committed by the applicant" (para 48); and it is clear from para 51 of its judgment that in coming to the conclusion that the applicant's deportation was disproportionate it took into account the fact that his sentence was comparatively low. Since it was established in **KO** that the relative seriousness of the offence cannot be taken into account in considering Exception 2 , it must be capable of being deployed by the potential deportee at the second stage.

Obviously it cannot be the case that an individual can rely on the fact that his offence attracted a sentence of, say, "only" twelve months as sufficient *by itself* to constitute very compelling circumstances for the purpose of section 117C(6): that would wholly subvert the statutory scheme. But if there were other compelling circumstances in his case the fact that his offence was comparatively less serious could form an element in his overall case that the strong public interest in deportation was outweighed.

Rehabilitation

This has long taken a back seat in non-EU deportations, but the judgment in **HA (Iraq)** brings it back to the fore. The court concluded:

> *What those authorities seem to me to establish is that the fact that a potential deportee has shown positive evidence of rehabilitation, and thus of a reduced risk of re-offending, cannot be excluded from the overall proportionality exercise. The authorities say so, and it must be right in principle in view of the holistic nature of that exercise. Where a tribunal is able to make an assessment that the foreign criminal is unlikely to re-offend, that is a factor which can carry some weight in the balance when considering very compelling circumstances. The weight which it will bear will vary from case to case, but it will rarely be of great weight bearing in mind that, as Moore-Bick LJ says in* ***Danso****, the public interest in the deportation of criminals is not based only on the need to protect the public from further offending by the foreign criminal in question but also on wider policy considerations of deterrence and public concern. I would add that tribunals will properly be cautious about their ability to make findings on the risk of re-offending, and will usually be unable to do so with any confidence based on no more than the undertaking of prison courses or mere assertions of reform by the offender or the absence of subsequent offending for what will typically be a relatively short period.*

CHAPTER SIX

REFUGEE CONVENTION CASES

In accordance with paragraph 397 of the Immigration Rules, in addition to being unable to sign a deportation order if removal of the person would be contrary to the UK's obligations under the Human Rights Convention, a deportation order can also not be issued if removal of the individual concerned would be unlawful under the Refugee Convention. This is also a statutory exception to deportation under Section 33(2) of the UK Borders Act. Unlike human rights based arguments under Article 8 ECHR, the Immigration Rules do not include a complete code for the consideration of arguments under the Refugee Convention; rather, you would need to satisfy to a relatively low standard of proof (a reasonable degree of likelihood) that your client will face persecution or serious harm upon return to their country of nationality, and that they wouldn't be able to secure protection from the authorities in their own country.

This is not a guide about asylum claims, so we will not be undertaking an in-depth review of asylum procedure in the UK, but it is important that advisors secure instructions about any potential Refugee Convention claim. As always, such a claim will need to be accompanied by evidence of the claimed persecution / protection available, including evidence about why your client will not be able to internally relocate to escape the threat. Furthermore, it is important to remember that a delay in making the claim may lead the Secretary of State to doubt your client's credibility (Section 8 of the Asylum and Immigration (Treatment of Claimants, etc.) Act 2004).

One further important point to remember when preparing deportation cases relying on refugee arguments is that certain individuals may be excluded from relying on the Refugee Convention under Article 1F of the Refugee Convention, Article 14(5) of the Qualification Direction or Article 33(2) of the Refugee Convention. These provisions exclude certain individuals from seeking refugee protection, but there will need to be serious reasons to believe that an individual has:

- Committed a crime against peace, a war crime, or a crime against humanity
- Committed a serious non-political crime outside the UK (country of refuge) prior to admission as a refugee
- Been found guilty of acts contrary to the purposes and principles of the United Nations

CHAPTER SEVEN

EEA DEPORTATION

EEA deportation cases are very different to deportation cases involving the deportation of non-EEA citizens. EEA law is much more flexible, and it should be easier to succeed with an EEA deportation case as opposed to a deportation case pursued under the Immigration Rules. It would, therefore, be beneficial to your client if you can prove that the case falls for consideration under EU law.

Despite Brexit, EU deportation law continues to apply to a number of cases, and it's likely that EEA deportation cases will continue to arise for years to come. Indeed, we anticipate this being a growth area for immigration practitioners, as citizens of these countries come up against domestic deportation rules for the first time. In this chapter, we will explain which potential deportees can and cannot benefit from EU law, and how to prepare a strong case against deportation on behalf of your clients.

Who can benefit from EU law?

Conduct pre 23:00 GMT on 31 December 2020

Despite the UK's departure from the EU, existing EU legislation, which includes provisions from the Immigration (European Economic Area) Regulations 2016, remain in force. The Regulations contain public policy, public security and public health tests; these continue to apply to deportation cases where the criminal activity occurred prior to the specified date (prior to 23:00 GMT on 31 December 2020).

Those who can benefit from the public policy, public security and public health tests in their deportation cases include those who:

- Have been granted permission to enter or remain in the UK under Appendix EU or Appendix EU (Family Permit). This applies to both EEA nationals and their family members, so is regardless of nationality.

- Were lawfully resident in the UK in accordance with the Immigration (EEA) Regulations 2016 by 23:00 GMT on 31 December 2020, again regardless of nationality.

- Are the family member of a person who was lawfully resident in the UK in accordance with the EEA Regulations 2016 by 23:00 GMT on 31 December 2020, even if they were not physically present in the UK by 23:00 GMT on 31 December 2020.

- Are a frontier worker in accordance with Regulation 3 of the Citizens Rights (Frontier Workers) (EU Exit) Regulations 2020.

- With reference to Appendix Service Providers from Switzerland of the Immigration Rules, are seeking permission to enter the UK/are already present in the UK as a service provider from Switzerland.

- Have or are seeking permission to enter/remain in the UK as a patient for the purpose of completing a course of planned healthcare treatment in the UK authorised under the S2 arrangements, as provided by Appendix S2 Healthcare Visitor to the Immigration Rules. This provision also includes persons or family members accompanying or joining the patient

For those who need to prove they were lawfully resident in the UK in accordance with the 2016 Regulations, it is important to remember that, under the Regulations, the EEA national must be undertaking a qualifying activity in the UK. The requirement to undertake a qualifying activity is largely redundant now due to Brexit; even if you can't prove lawful residence under the 2016 Regulations, if the EEA national was present in the UK prior to 23:00 GMT on 31 December 2020, they should still be able to qualify for leave to remain in the UK under Appendix EU of the Immigration Rules.

For those who aren't EEA nationals, you'll need evidence to prove that they were the family member of an EEA national and that the EEA national was undertaking a qualifying activity in the UK (in accordance with the 2016 regulations) or was simply present in the UK prior to 23:00 GMT on 31 December 2020 (in accordance with Appendix EU of the Immigration Rules). Remember that extended family members will only be lawfully present in the UK if they held a residence document issued on the basis of their relationship with their EEA national family member; this document would need to be issued prior to 23:00 GMT for them to be able to prove they were lawfully present in the UK on this date. Only if a residence document has been issued can they prove that they were lawfully resident in the UK.

If an EEA national or their family member ceases to have a right to reside under the 2016 Regulations and they cannot qualify for permission to stay under Appendix EU, they may not qualify for consideration with reference to the public policy, public security and public health tests.

Conduct post 23:00 GMT on 31 December 2020

In cases where the criminal activity was committed after 31 December 2020, the Secretary of State will consider whether deportation is justified on the ground that it is conducive to the public good (with reference to s3(5) of the Immigration Act 1971), or on the ground that deportation has been recommended by a court (s3(6) Immigration Act 1971). In our experience, courts rarely recommend deportation, but even if they did, their recommendation alone doesn't justify the issuing of a deportation decision; the Secretary of State would, however, need to consider the recommendation and conclude whether deportation is justified.

As noted earlier in this guide, the UK Borders Act 2007 has also been amended, meaning the automatic provisions can also apply to EEA nationals who commit an offence after 23:00 GMT on 31 December 2020. The inclusion of EEA nationals means that an additional exception to deportation has been specified at s33(4); the automatic deportation provisions will not apply to those who were lawfully resident in the UK in accordance with EU Treaties immediately before commencement day, or who have permission to reside in the UK by virtue of Appendix EU of the Immigration Rules.

Conduct pre 23:00 GMT on 31 December 2020 and post 23:00 GMT on 31 December

If criminal conduct occurred both before and after 23:00 GMT on 31 December 2020, the public policy, public security or public health test can still apply. The Secretary of State will need to decide whether to consider the totality of the conduct under the public policy, public security or public health tests under the Regulations, or whether to consider only the conduct that occurred after 31 December. If the latter, the conduct that occurred after 31 December 2020 will be considered on the ground that deportation is conducive to the public good, and the pre 31 December 2020 conduct will not form part of the deportation decision (it will not be considered with reference to the conducive to the public good test, or the public policy, public security or public health tests). It would, of course, be open to the Secretary of State to try to rely on pre 31 December conduct with reference to the individual's character and risk of reoffending.

Definition of committed

For the purpose of these provisions, at the date of writing this guide, there isn't a clear definition of what is meant by conduct committed pre or post 31 December. Our initial thoughts are that, as long as the criminal activity (the conduct) was committed pre 23:00 GMT on 31 December 2020, it shouldn't matter that the conviction occurred after 23:00 GMT on 31 December. However, there's likely to be litigation on this point, so watch this space. For now, we definitely think it's worth arguing that the EEA provisions apply in cases where the offending was pre 31 December, even if the conviction occurs after the specified date. In our opinion, the date an offence is committed is different to the date an offender is convicted; if the Secretary of State only wanted the EEA deportation provisions to apply to those who were convicted before 23:00 GMT on 31 December 2020, then surely she would have used the word convicted as opposed to committed.

Irish nationals

Irish nationals, as EEA nationals, can be deported from the UK, but deportations are extremely rare. This is because, on 19 February 2007, the then Home Secretary, John Reid, announced in Parliament that the UK would not deport Irish citizens unless exceptional circumstances existed or if deportation was recommended by a court. This announcement was made to maintain the position that the rights of British and Irish citizens should be protected when in each other's states. The UK Borders Act 2007 (s32) has been amended to confirm that, similar to a British citizen, Irish citizens cannot meet the definition of a foreign criminal and thus cannot be deported with reference to the automatic provisions.

Relevant legislation

If you have now identified that your client may be able to benefit from EU law, it is worthwhile understanding a background to the legislation, just in case it needs be quoted in your EEA representations, grounds of appeal or skeleton arguments. We have already explained that provisions from the 2016 Regulations will continue to apply despite Brexit, so we will now explain why these provisions continue to apply to certain EEA deportation cases.

The European Union (Withdrawal Agreement) Act 2020, along with various secondary legislation, confirmed that certain provisions contained in the 2016 Regulations will continue post the end of the Brexit transition period. The legislation has also modified some of the provisions that apply post 31 December.

One of the provisions retained was Regulation 27 of the 2016 Regulations. Regulation 27 enables the Secretary of State to issue a decision on public policy, public security or public health grounds, and it sets out the relevant tests that must be met before the Secretary of State can issue such a decision. If Regulation 27 applies, with reference to Regulation 23(5), the Secretary of State can issue an *exclusion* decision which will prevent the individual from returning to the UK. If they want to return to the UK, or if they remain in the UK and want confirmation of their right to remain in the UK, the exclusion (also known as deportation) decision would need to be revoked.

Due to Brexit, legislation was enacted to ensure that the public policy, public security and public health tests continue to apply in cases where criminal activity was committed before 23:00 GMT on 31 December 2020. As this may need to be referenced in future deportation cases, it is summarised as follows:

- The Grace Period Regulations 2020 impose the 30 June 2021 deadline for applications under the EU Settlement Scheme (EUSS). They also protect the existing rights of individuals who were present in the UK prior to the end of the transition period, but who do not yet hold a document under the EUSS.
- The Restrictions Regulations 2020 save and modify the deportation provisions in the EEA Regulations 2016. These Regulations enable the public policy, public security or public health test to continue to apply to conduct committed before 23:00 GMT on 31 December 2020.
- The Frontier Workers Regulations 2020 extend the deportation provisions to frontier workers who were in the UK prior to 31 December 2020. Frontier workers are EU nationals resident in another EU state who regularly travel to the UK to work; their permanent home must not be in the UK.
- Under the Immigration Rules:
    - Appendix EU
    - Appendix S2 Healthcare Visitor
    - Appendix Service Providers from Switzerland

A deportation order cannot actually be issued under Appendix EU of the Immigration Rules, but Appendix EU does confirm that indefinite leave to enter or remain, which has been issued under the EUSS, can be revoked if a person is liable to deportation but cannot be deported for legal reasons. Appendix EU also contains various definitions in relation to deportation, as the Appendix confirms that those who are the subject

of a deportation order will not be suitable for leave to remain, and also that a deportation order may break continuous residence.
In addition to the above provisions, a plethora of case law exists in relation to how the public policy, public security and public health tests are applied. This is summarised below and will hopefully assist with representing clients before the Home Office or Tribunal.

When can an EEA national be deported – conduct pre-23:00 GMT on 31 December 2020

As mentioned previously, for criminal conduct which pre-dates the end of the transition period, the Secretary of State can seek to deport EEA nationals from the UK on grounds of public policy, public security and public health. The grounds on which a decision can be issued will depend on the individual's length of residence in the UK; the longer they have been present in the UK, the more difficult it is to remove them from the UK. Regulation 27 confirms the grounds on which a deportation order can be signed:

- If the individual has been present in the UK for less than five years, grounds of public policy, public security or public health must exist.

- If they hold permanent residence (have resided in the UK for at least five years), a deportation decision can only be issued if serious grounds of public policy and public security exist.

- If they have been present in the UK for a continuous period of ten years or are under the age of 18 (unless issuing a deportation decision is in the best interests of the child), a deportation decision can only be issued if imperative grounds of public security exist.

It is important to secure full instructions from a client in relation to their residence in the UK; the longer you can prove they have been lawfully resident in the UK, the more difficult it will be to deport them.

Although Appendix EU removed the need to provide evidence of a qualifying activity, as residence may pre-date the introduction of Appendix EU on 28 August 2018 and because the Regulations (as opposed to Appendix EU will apply to the consideration of the case), it will still be necessary to provide evidence of qualifying activities. When securing instructions, you should, therefore, secure instructions in relation the EEA national's activities in the UK.

Continuity of residence

The serious and imperative grounds tests require continuous residence for either five or ten years. Regulation 3 of the 2016 Regulations defines continuity of residence, with similar provisions being contained in Appendix EU. The Regulations confirm that continuity of residence will be affected by periods of absence which exceed six months in total in any year. Continuity of residence will not, however, be affected if an absence is necessary due to compulsory military service, or if one absence is less than twelve months but is for an important reason such as pregnancy, childbirth, serious illness, study or vocational training or an overseas posting.

As a result of the Coronavirus pandemic, the Secretary of State has confirmed that continuity of residence will not be affected if an individual could not return to the UK due to coronavirus restrictions. However, the absence – even if travel couldn't be arranged due to coronavirus restrictions – must not exceed twelve months. For those who have been absent for more than twelve months, in order not to break continuity of residence and to continue to rely on EU law for pre 23:00 GMT 31 December 2020 criminal conduct, they will need to have returned to the UK by 23:00 GMT on 31 December.

Imprisonment usually breaks continuity of residence, so it is important to try to evidence the relevant five- or ten-year period prior to the custodial sentence being imposed. There is, however, additional protection for those who have completed ten years residence in the UK. With reference to Regulation 3(4), an EEA national or their family member, may be able to argue that imprisonment hasn't broken their continuity of residence, if they have lived in the UK continuously and lawfully for ten years and they can prove that they had forged integrating links with the UK prior to imprisonment; imprisonment hasn't broken those integrating links; and it would not be appropriate to assert that the sentence of imprisonment has broken continuity of residence.

The longer you can prove that an EEA national or their family member has continuously and lawfully resided in the UK for, the easier it will be to argue that their deportation from the UK will be unlawful.

Qualifying activity

As mentioned earlier in this book, although the EUSS doesn't require evidence of an EEA national's qualifying activity, as the 2016 Regulations will apply, it is likely that we will be required to evidence lawful residence in accordance with the Regulations. This is especially so if trying to prove lawful residence over five or ten years. Such lawful residence would need to comply with the 2016 Regulations, so this would involve proving qualifying activities (for the EEA national) and relationship to the EEA national (for family members). Such evidence should cover the period of residence relied upon.

If dealing with a case where someone has completed ten years residence in the UK, you would only need to provide evidence of continuous qualifying activity for five years; after five years, the EEA national / their family members would have acquired permanent residence, so you'd approach their lawful residence on the following basis:

- Provide evidence of qualifying activity for five continuous years – the individual then acquired permanent residence with reference to Regulation 15 of the 2016 Regulations.

- For the remaining five years, the individual was lawfully present in the UK as an EEA national / a family member of an EEA national who held permanent residence – no evidence of qualifying activity is required, as someone who holds permanent residence is lawfully present in the UK. Evidence of continuity of residence will, however, be necessary.

Qualifying activities include being a:

- Jobseeker
- Worker
- Self-employed person
- Self-sufficient (access to sufficient resources to not become a burden on the social assistance system, and comprehensive sickness insurance)
- Student (studying a course, has access to sufficient resources not to become a burden on the social assistance system, and has comprehensive sickness insurance)

As this is a guide concentrating on deportation provisions, we will not be providing an in-depth review of qualifying activities. It should, however, be noted that activities should be continuous, and evidence should be continuous, with no more than 6-month gaps in-between evidence. Remember that there are circumstances when an EEA national can cease to undertake a qualifying activity and will still be lawfully present in the UK. These are outlined at Regulation 5 of the 2016 Regulations, and apply to workers or self-employed persons who have ceased activity due to retirement or permanent incapacity to work. Such individuals will have needed to have completed work or self-employment in the UK continuously for twelve months prior to termination and must have resided in the UK continuously for at least twelve months. Provisions also apply for those resident in the UK, but who undertake employment or self-employment in another EEA state.

Grounds of public policy, public security and public health

This is the lowest level of protection that can be afforded to an EEA national or their family member. It applies to adults who do not hold permanent residence (have not been in the UK lawfully for five years).

Although this is the lowest level of protection available, it's important to remember that there must be a present threat to the interests of society;

a historic criminal record / historic threat is not in itself sufficient to justify deportation. This was made clear at paragraph 16 of the Court of Appeal decision in **Bulale v SSHD [2008] EWCA Civ 806**. As outlined below, the burden of proving a genuine, present and sufficiently serious threat under Regulation 27(5) rests on the Secretary of State.

Obviously, the longer your client has been in the UK, the more difficult it will be to deport them from the UK, so if you can prove that the additional levels of protection apply, arguments of this nature should be included in your representations to the Home Office and Tribunal.

Serious grounds of public policy and public security

The Regulations do not define what amounts to serious grounds of public policy and public security, but to reflect the additional level of protection, these cases must be more serious than those involving an individual who has not acquired permanent residence. Determining whether serious grounds exist will involve an assessment of the seriousness of the offence, and how involved with the criminal activities the individual was.

The nature of the crime is relevant; at paragraph 28 of **Bulale** the Court of Appeal acknowledged that it should be *"...difficult to expel an EU citizen on the basis of crimes of dishonesty, but that violence is a different matter."* It's therefore likely to be difficult to argue that serious grounds do not exist in cases involving violence, including those involving drugs, where the Secretary of State is likely to argue that a large number of people were likely to be affected by the offending.

Imperative grounds of public security

This is the highest level of protection that can be afforded to an EEA national, and it will be very difficult for the Secretary of State to deport an EEA national from the UK if this test applies.

Once again, imperative grounds are not defined in the EEA Regulations 2016 or the Directive. In accordance with the Secretary of State's guidance[1], the term may be interpreted more widely than threats to the state or its institutions, and imperative grounds can exist in serious criminality cases, such as drug dealing as part of an organised group.

Caselaw confirms that imperative grounds can only exist in the most serious matters. In **MG and VC (Ireland) [2006] UKAIT 00053**, the Tribunal confirmed that the imperative grounds test is at the very highest level of the calculus introduced by the 2006 Regulations and Directive 2004/38/EC, thus highlighting that the threshold is very high. In **VP (Italy) v SSHD [2010] EWCA Civ 806**, the Court provided more guidance on just how high this level is, concluding that the imperative grounds test requires an actual risk to public security so compelling that it justifies the exceptional removal of someone who has become integrated.

In **LG (Italy) [2008] EWCA Civ 90**, the court concluded that imperative grounds can exist in offences involving the commission of terrorism, to those involving serious criminal offending to include murder, drug trafficking, serious sexual or violent offending. The court acknowledged that the imperative grounds test should be narrower and more stringent, when compared to the lower levels of protection.

Tsakouridis (European Citizenship) [2010] EUECJ C-145/09 is a German case which involved a request for a preliminary ruling from the ECJ. It is referenced in the Secretary of State's EEA deportation policy guidance. The ECJ found that imperative grounds cases are not reserved solely to the cases involving threats to the state or its institutions. Rather, imperative (and serious) grounds may exist in serious criminal cases, such as drug dealing as part of an organised group. As the Secretary of State is likely to rely on **Tsakouridis** in their deportation decisions, it is worthwhile understanding the facts of the case, so that you can distinguish the case from your own.

---

[1] https://assets.publishing.service.gov.uk/government/uploads/system/uploads/attachment_data/file/668087/EEA-Decisions-taken-on-grounds-of-public-policy-3.0EXT.pdf

Mr Tsakouridis, a citizen of Greece, had resided in Germany for more than 20 years. He received a custodial sentence of six years and six months after being convicted of eight counts of illegal dealing in substantial quantities of narcotics as part of an organised group. He also had various other offences for which he had previously received fines. These offences included: possession of a prohibited object, dangerous assault, intentional assault and compulsion, and compulsion and intentional assault. Mr Tsakouridis' case was, therefore, serious, and in addition to being involved with narcotics, he was part of an organised group who likely sold a substantial quantity of narcotics – it wasn't low level dealing.

In **P.I (Imperative grounds of public security) [2009] EUECJ C-348-09**, another case referenced in the Secretary of State's guidance, the ECJ found that Member States could consider that the crimes referenced in the second paragraph of Article 83(1) of the Treaties of the European Union (TFEU) are capable of meeting the imperative grounds of public security threshold. These include the following crimes: terrorism, trafficking in human beings and sexual exploitation of women and children, illicit drug trafficking, illicit arms trafficking, money laundering, corruption, counterfeiting of means of payment, computer crime and organised crime.

In **P.I** the ECJ further concluded that, whether an Article 83(1) offence would meet the imperative grounds threshold will depend on the manner in which the offence was committed, and whether the offence concerned particularly serious characteristics. P.I is not, therefore, a blanket policy which confirms that all Article 83(1) cases amount to imperative grounds. To justify exclusion on imperative grounds, the personal conduct of the individual concerned must represent a genuine, present threat which affects one of the fundamental interests of society or of the host Member State. Therefore, in addition to committing an Article 83(1) offence in a serious manner, the individual facing deportation must show a propensity to act in the same way in the future. The Member State must also consider the Regulation 27(5) and 27(6) factors (outlined below).

There are also a number of cases which highlight that imperative grounds only exist in limited cases, and that the threshold can only be met in the most serious of matters. For example, in **Secretary of State for the Home Department v FV (Italy) [2012] EWCA Civ 1199**, a serious offence of violence which resulted in a custodial sentence of 8 years did not justify deportation on imperative grounds of public security. In **Jarusevicius (EEA Reg 21 – effect of imprisonment) [2012] UKUT 001200 (IAC)**, it was held that a 42-month prison sentence for handling stolen goods and a previous sentence for driving while drunk did not meet imperative grounds.

Furthermore, in **Capparrelli (EEA Nationals – British Nationality) [2017] UKUT 00162 (IAC)**, the Upper Tribunal found that a series of criminal offences, including offences against the person, criminal damage, harassment and the index conviction of rape, did not overcome the threshold of imperative public security. In **Capparrelli**, the Appellant had served a 2-year prison sentence for assault occasioning actual bodily harm, before receiving a 6.5-year sentence for rape, yet the First-tier and Upper Tribunals both confirmed that imperative grounds did not exist.

The threshold of the imperative grounds test is clearly an exceptional one which requires extremely serious criminality, involving offences against the state, such as terrorism, or serious illegal drug dealing as part of an organised group.

Other factors relevant to EEA deportation cases

Regulation 27(5) confirms that, before issuing a deportation decision, the Secretary of State must consider the following principles:

- Whether the decision is proportionate
- The decision must be based exclusively on the personal conduct of the person concerned
- The personal conduct of the person concerned must represent a genuine, present and sufficiently serious threat affecting one of the fundamental interests of society, taking into account past conduct of the person concerned. The threat does not need to be imminent. Schedule 1 to the 2016 Regulations and the Schedule

to the Frontier Workers Regulations 2020 provides non-exhaustive lists of what is meant by the fundamental interests of society. They include:

- Preventing unlawful immigration and abuse of immigration laws, in order to maintain the integrity and effectiveness of the immigration control system.
- Maintaining public order.
- Preventing social harm.
- Preventing the evasion of tax and duties.
- Protecting public services.
- Excluding or removing a relevant person with a conviction, and maintaining public confidence in the ability of the relevant authorities to take such action
- Tackling offences likely to cause harm to society, for example drugs and those offences reference at paragraph 2 of Article 83(1) TFEU.

As was made clear by the Upper Tribunal in **Arranz (EEA Regulations – deportation – test) [2017] UKUT 00294 (IAC)**, the burden of proving a genuine, present and sufficiently serious threat rests on the Secretary of State. The standard of proof is the balance of probabilities.

Returning to the Regulation 27(5) considerations:

- Matters isolated from the particulars of the case or which relate to considerations of general prevention do not justify the decision.
- Previous criminal convictions do not in themselves justify the decision.
- The decision may be taken on preventative grounds, even in the absence of a previous criminal conviction, provided the grounds are specific to the person.

Schedule 1 to the 2016 Regulations also outlines various other considerations, relevant to public policy and public security. For example, an EEA national who has extensive links with persons of the same nationality or language would not be considered to be integrated in the UK, and little weight should be attached to integration if links were formed around the same time as the offending. A helpful consideration is outlined at paragraph 5 of Schedule 1, which confirms that removal of someone who can provide substantive evidence that they do not pose a threat is less likely to be proportionate. Strong evidence of the threat your client poses is therefore necessary, and it may be worthwhile instructing an independent expert to comment on their risk.

Relevant to the consideration of whether a decision is proportionate is the Upper Tribunal case of **Essa (EEA: rehabilitation/integration** [2013] **UKUT 00316 (IAC).** The matter had previously been before the Court of Appeal (**R (Essa) v Upper Tribunal (Immigration & Asylum Chamber)** [2012] **EWCA Civ 1718**). The Court of Appeal held that a decision maker must consider whether deportation will prejudice the prospects of rehabilitation, and that this consideration is relevant to the proportionality exercise. This will entail a comparison with the prospects in the home country and requires a broad interpretation of rehabilitation. The social and family support available is as important as the more formal structures. When the case returned to the Upper Tribunal, the panel considered further the significance of rehabilitation on the proportionality assessment and held that prospects of rehabilitation are a substantial relevant factor in the proportionality balance when considering whether deportation is justified. There are helpful considerations contained in the headnote which can be copied into representations/skeleton arguments.

Propensity to offend is also relevant to the above considerations; evidence relating to a client's risk of reoffending and threat to the public is important. This information is usually contained in a pre-sentence or OASys report, but an expert can also be instructed, especially if the offending is historic. In addition to these reports, evidence about a client's change in character would help to overturn a conclusion that imperative grounds exist. This could perhaps include evidence of any courses they have completed, charitable activities etc.

Regulation 27(6) provides further factors that must be taken into account before a deportation decision is issued:

- Age
- State of health
- Family and economic situation
- Length of UK residence
- Social and cultural integration into the UK
- Extent of links with country of origin

In addition to the above factors, all decisions must, of course, be in the best interests of any children that it affects, so as is the case with all immigration decisions, it is important to consider the impact a deportation decision will have on any children it affects. See earlier in this book, where this is considered in further detail.

Specifically applicable to EEA deportation cases are those who hold a right to reside with reference to **Ruiz Zambrano (European Citizenship) [2011] EUECJ C-3409.** As many practitioners will be aware, **Zambrano** established that a non-EU parent of an EU citizen child may be entitled to a right to reside in the EU, if the refusal of a right to reside would force the child to leave the EU and subsequently deprive them of their right to live in the EU as an EU citizen. If a Zambrano application was successful under the Regulations, the non-EU national parent would receive a derivative right of residence. Even if a non-EU national holds a derivative right of residence, the Secretary of State can still seek to deport them from the UK, so it's important to carefully evidence relationships with British/EU children, and to consider whether that child will be deprived of UK/EU residence if their parent is deported. If the parent facing deportation has spent time with custody, who took care of the child while they were in custody, and could the child continue to live with that family member / friend / carer? An independent social worker report may assist here, to comment on how the child has coped during the parent's imprisonment, whether the child would be affected by continuing the current living situation with their parent deported, and why it would be in the child's best interests for their parent to continue to live in the UK.

Conduct post 31 December 2020 – not conducive to the public good

As noted above, the automatic deportation provisions under the UK Borders Act 2007 may apply, but only if the offender was not lawfully resident in the UK by 31 December 2020 in accordance with the 2016 Regulations or Appendix EU.

If your client qualifies for an exception to automatic deportation, as noted above, before issuing a decision on the basis that the individual's continued presence is not conducive to the public good, a balancing exercise must be undertaken. The decision-maker must set out the reasons why an individual's continued presence may be considered to be non-conducive, and must then weigh these reasons against the factors indicating why deportation may be disproportionate.

When setting out the reasons an individual's presence may be non-conducive, the Secretary of State will consider:

- Court recommendation for deportation
- Seriousness of the offence – serious drug offences or gun crime are likely to result in an assertion that continued presence is not conducive to the public good
- Length of sentence – if more than 12 months likely to be seen as non-conducive, although if the offence is serious (has caused serious harm, for example) and the individual received a sentence of less than 12 months, the Secretary of State may still assert that continued presence is not conducive to the public good
- Persistent offending – in other words a repeat offender who has shown a pattern of offending over a period of time

In addition to considering the offence in question, the decision-maker can also take into account cautions and previous convictions. This means that, if offending occurred both before and after 23:00 GMT on 31

December 2020, even if the Secretary of State opts to consider post 31 December conduct with reference to the conducive grounds test, she will also be able to reference pre 31 December conduct, although this alone shouldn't be the sole reason to justify deportation.

Relevant factors when considering whether deportation would be disproportionate will include:

- Length of UK residence
- Ties to the UK
- UK's obligations under the human rights convention
- UK's obligations under the refugee convention

When addressing conducive grounds decision making at the date of publishing this book, the Secretary of State refers to her own guidance: Deport-non eea Foreign Nationals.pdf (publishing.service.gov.uk). Section 3 of this guidance solely considers the relevant test, but is not extensive. When considering human rights arguments, the Secretary of State will consider paragraph 398 of the Immigration Rules, as discussed in detail in earlier chapters.

Arguments with reference to the Refugee Convention can also be made, but it is likely to be rare that a refugee convention case will arise in EEA deportation cases, although potentially could for a non-EEA family member.

EEA Procedure

If the Secretary of State considers that an EEA national is liable to deportation, they must notify the individual in writing. This must inform the individual that they are being considered for deportation, and must give them an opportunity to provide reasons/documents in relation to why they should not be deported. The Secretary of State will then consider the individual's response before issuing their final decision.

If a deportation decision is made in relation to pre-31 December 2020 conduct, the decision will attract an in-country right of appeal. However, with reference to Regulation 33 of the 2016 Regulations, that decision may be certified, having the effect that the person can be removed pending their appeal. Similar to s94B certifications considered earlier in this book, Regulation 33 confirms that an individual who is subject to an EEA exclusion/deportation decision may be removed from the UK before the appeal has been finally determined, if the Secretary of State certifies that their removal pending the outcome of the appeal would not be unlawful under s6 of the Human Rights Act 1998. Regulation 33(3) enables the decision-maker to rely on the ground that the individual would not, before the appeal is finally determined, face a real risk of serious irreversible harm if removed from the UK.

An interim order can be applied for in an attempt to suspend removal, but if the Secretary of State is considering removal pending the final hearing, it is extremely difficult to suspend such a removal, especially if the decision concerns an EEA national. This is because an EEA national can easily return to the UK to attend their hearing. In **R (Wandzel) v Secretary of State for the Home Department (Rev 1) [2018] EWHC 1371 (Admin)**, the Administrative Court considered Regulation 33. Mr Wandzel sought to argue that the certification applied to his case under Regulation 33 was unlawful. Mr Wandzel's case was dismissed, largely due to his EU nationality and his ability to return to the UK to provide oral evidence at his appeal hearing. The court concluded that he could easily contact his legal representatives in the UK; it wouldn't be difficult for him to make the reasonably short trip back to the UK from Poland to give evidence at his hearing; and also because Mr Wandzel's offending wasn't especially serious. He was a persistent offender, but had never actually served a prison sentence of more than a day.

Gheorghiu (reg 24AA EEA Regs – relevant factors) [2016] UKUT 00024 (IAC) is relevant for those who may want to seek an interim order to prevent removal pending the hearing. In this case, the Upper Tribunal confirmed the factors that a judge should take into account when considering whether to suspend removal pre-appeal. The factors are outlined at paragraph 22 of the judgement.

For post-31 December 2020 conduct, although we're yet to come across such cases, it is expected that the same appeal rights that apply to non-EEA cases will apply, as discussed in this book.

The deportation order may be issued at the same time as the deportation decision, or may be issued on a later date. If the Home Office does not remove an individual from the UK within two years of issuing their deportation order, the decision to deport will need to be reconsidered.

CHAPTER EIGHT

MANAGING LITIGATION

The Secretary of State's decision to make a deportation order (i.e. their consideration of the human rights arguments advanced above) will attract a right of appeal before the First-tier Tribunal. The appeal can be brought while the individual is present in the UK unless the claim is certified under s94B of the Nationality, Immigration and Asylum Act 2002 (as amended by the Immigration Act 2014).

Section 94B is a discretionary power enabling the Secretary of State to remove an Appellant from the UK before his appeal is concluded. It came into force on 28 July 2014 and applies only to those liable to deportation who have made a human rights claim. The provision does not apply to those who have submitted an asylum or humanitarian claim, although such claims can be certified with reference to ss94 and 96 of the NIAA 2002. Section 94 would apply if the Secretary of State considers the claim is unfounded; it can apply to both asylum and human rights claims, but in practice s94B is relied on in human rights cases. S96 can be relied upon if the Appellant has previously been notified of a right of appeal, and the claim to which the new decision relates relies on a ground that could have been raised in the earlier claim. The Secretary of State must also be satisfied that there is no satisfactory reason for the ground not having been raised in the previous appeal. In practice, s96 is rarely used.

A decision can be certified under Section 94B if the Secretary of State considers that the removal of the individual pending the outcome of their appeal would not be unlawful under s6 of the HRA 1998. Section 94B(3) confirms that the Secretary of State can certify a claim if the individual would not face a real risk of serious irreversible harm if removed from the UK before the appeal is concluded, but this is not the sole reason under which a s94B certificate can be issued; other factors are also relevant to the consideration of whether removal would be unlawful under s6 of the HRA 1998.

The application of Section 94B came before the Supreme Court in **R (on the applications of Kiarie and Byndloss) v SSHD [2017] UKSC 42.** In this case, the Supreme Court considered the difficulties faced by non-EEA Appellants who were trying to exercise their appeal while they were outside of the UK. The court concluded that for an appeal to be effective, an Appellant must be afforded an opportunity to give live evidence (paragraph 76), and that the financial and logistical barriers involved with enabling the Appellants to give live evidence on screen was insurmountable. The Court concluded that the s94B certificates issued by the Secretary of State breached the procedural requirements of Article 8.

Section 94B was under scrutiny again by the Upper Tribunal in **AJ (s 94B: Kiarie and Byndloss questions) Nigeria [2018] UKUT 00115 (IAC).** In this case, the Upper Tribunal issued guidance confirming the factors to be taken into account when considering whether an out-of-country appeal is adequate, thus confirming that not all out-of-country appeals will be unlawful. These are summarised at paragraph 2 of the headnote, and essentially involve an assessment of: having the ability to secure legal representations, whether absence from the UK will impair the Appellant's ability to produce expert/professional evidence, whether it is necessary to heave live evidence from the Appellant, and whether such evidence can be heard via videolink. The Appellant in **AJ** was a citizen of Nigeria, and the matter was remitted to the First-tier Tribunal for them to consider the factors outlined above.

It is important to remember that, if challenging a certification decision, representatives should also consider a challenge to possible unlawful detention. Detention could be unlawful if the certification decision is unlawful; the Secretary of State cannot reasonably expect to remove an individual from the UK if the certification decision requiring their removal is unlawful.

It has been Home Office practice for some years to pursue deportation action against foreign criminals in a particularly vigorous manner. If the Secretary of State loses an appeal at first instance, an application for permission to appeal to the Upper Tribunal is almost inevitable. If they lose again, an application to the Court of Appeal is likely to be made.

In our view, courts and tribunals have been overly receptive to such applications by the Secretary of State in recent years, frequently overturning apparently sustainable decisions of the First tier Tribunal on grounds that amount to mere disagreement with the factual outcome to a case. The Court of Appeal does however seem to be increasingly alive to this problem, and in cases such as **Lowe v SSHD [2021] EWCA Civ 62** has deprecated the Upper Tribunal's willingness to revisit factual findings in the First tier based on its own assessment of the evidence in deportation cases.

In this regard, reliance may be placed on the judgment of Lewison LJ in **Fage UK Ltd. v Chobani UK Ltd. [2014] EWCA Civ 5** at paras 114-5:

> *114. Appellate courts have been repeatedly warned, by recent cases at the highest level, not to interfere with findings of fact by trial judges, unless compelled to do so. This applies not only to findings of primary fact, but also to the evaluation of those facts and to inferences to be drawn from them. The best known of these cases are: Biogen Inc v Medeva Plc [1997] RPC 1 ; Piglowska v Piglowski [1999] 1 WLR 1360 ; Datec Electronics Holdings Ltd v United Parcels Service Ltd [2007] UKHL 23; [2007] 1 WLR 1325 ; Re B (A Child) (Care Proceedings) [2013] UKSC 33; [2013] 1 WLR 1911 and most recently and comprehensively McGraddie v McGraddie [2013] UKSC 58; [2013] 1 WLR 2477 . These are all decisions either of the House of Lords or of the Supreme Court. The reasons for this approach are many. They include:*
>
> > *i. The expertise of a trial judge is in determining what facts are relevant to the legal issues to be decided, and what those facts are if they are disputed.*
> >
> > *ii. The trial is not a dress rehearsal. It is the first and last night of the show.*
> >
> > *iii. Duplication of the trial judge's role on appeal is a disproportionate use of the limited resources of an appellate court, and will seldom lead to a different outcome in an individual case.*

iv. In making his decisions the trial judge will have regard to the whole of the sea of evidence presented to him, whereas an appellate court will only be island hopping.

v. The atmosphere of the courtroom cannot, in any event, be recreated by reference to documents (including transcripts of evidence).

vi. Thus even if it were possible to duplicate the role of the trial judge, it cannot in practice be done.

115. It is also important to have in mind the role of a judgment given after trial. The primary function of a first instance judge is to find facts and identify the crucial legal points and to advance reasons for deciding them in a particular way. He should give his reasons in sufficient detail to show the parties and, if need be, the Court of Appeal the principles on which he has acted and the reasons that have led him to his decision. They need not be elaborate. There is no duty on a judge, in giving his reasons, to deal with every argument presented by counsel in support of his case. His function is to reach conclusions and give reasons to support his view, not to spell out every matter as if summing up to a jury. Nor need he deal at any length with matters that are not disputed. It is sufficient if what he says shows the basis on which he has acted.

CHAPTER NINE

REVOKING A DEPORTATION ORDER

An individual who is the subject of a deportation order cannot return to the UK whilst the order remains in force. Nor can they qualify for entry clearance or leave to remain (if they were never actually deported from the UK). Therefore, if they would like to return to the UK, the individual will need to apply to revoke the deportation first; only if they can revoke the deportation will they be able to apply for leave to enter or remain under our Immigration Rules. The requirements involved in revoking deportation orders are different, depending on whether the case involves a non-EEA or EEA (pre-31 December) deportation order.

Applications for revocation of a deportation order do not require the completion of an application form, nor payment of a fee; representations and supporting documentation may be provided to the Entry Clearance Officer or the Home Office in the UK. We usually submit representations to the Criminal Casework team in the UK who dealt with the deportation case. Decisions can take a long time to be issued, usually between six to twelve months in our experience. These cases are not treated as a priority by the Home Office.

If refused, the decision will attract a right of appeal on human rights grounds, unless certified.

Non-EEA

With reference to paragraph 362 of the Immigration Rules, non-EEA deportation orders prohibit the individual it is issued against from returning to the UK for as long as the order is in force. It also invalidates any leave to enter or remain that the individual held prior to the signing of the deportation order.

Section 32(6) of the UK Borders Act 2007 contains provisions in relation to when a deportation order issued under the Act (with reference to the automatic deportation provisions discussed earlier in this guide) can be revoked. These include:

- One of the Section 33 exceptions apply, as discussed earlier in this guide
- The application for revocation is made while the foreign criminal is outside of the UK
- If Section 34(4) of the 2007 Act applies – if the Secretary of State decides to take action under the Immigration Acts, and issue a new deportation decision with reference to Section 32(5) applies

When instructed to prepare an application to revoke a deportation order, the Immigration Rules will need to be considered. Paragraph 390 of the Immigration Rules outlines the information the Secretary of State will take into consideration when considering an application to revoke a deportation order. Before explaining the considerations in further detail, it is worthwhile considering the criteria outlined at paragraph 391, which explains how long a deportation order should ideally remain in force. Under paragraph 391:

- For someone who received a custodial sentence of less than four years, the Secretary of State expects the deportation order to remain in force for at least 10 years (calculated from the date the order was issued).
- For those who received a custodial sentence of at least four years, the deportation order can remain in force indefinitely.

For other cases, perhaps someone who was deported on grounds of being a persistent offender, so didn't complete a period in custody, with reference to paragraph 391A of the Immigration Rules, revocation will not normally be authorised unless the situation has materially changed, either by a change of circumstances since the order was made, or perhaps as a result of fresh evidence which was not previously relied upon. This paragraph of the Rules also acknowledges that passage of time itself can amount to a change of circumstance so as to result in the revocation of the order, but this would also require a lot of evidence about the individual's change of character.

The above are only guidelines; the Rules go on to confirm that, notwithstanding the expected duration of a deportation order, if continuation of the order is contrary to the Human Rights Convention or the Convention and Protocol Relating to the Status of Refugees, or if there are any other exceptional circumstances which mean that continuation is outweighed by compelling factors, an application to revoke the order can be submitted at any time. It will, of course, be more difficult to succeed with an application to revoke a deportation order for someone who received a custodial sentence of at least four years, or if ten years hasn't passed since the order issued against someone who received a custodial sentence of less than four years has not passed.

When considering paragraph 391 and the length of time that has passed since the deportation order was signed, the Upper Tribunal case of **Smith (paragraph 391(a) – revocation of deportation order)** [2017] **UKUT 00166 (IAC)** is useful. This acknowledges that, for those who received a custodial sentence of less than four years, if ten years has passed since the decision to make a deportation order, the public interest does not require continuation of the order. However, the Secretary of State is still permitted to consider each case, and can still maintain the order if there are strong public policy reasons to justify the maintenance of the order. The headnote is helpful, and should be copied into representations if applicable.

We'll now look at what factors the Secretary of State will take into account when considering whether to revoke a deportation order. As noted above, these are outlined at paragraph 390 of the Immigration Rules, and they include a consideration of:

- The reasons why the order was made;
- Representations made in support of the revocation application;
- The interests of the community, including the maintenance of an effective immigration control; and

- The interests of the individual, including any compassionate circumstances.

From experience, it is very difficult to revoke a non-EEA deportation order, especially if outside the ten year timeframe specified at paragraph 391 of the Immigration Rules. It isn't impossible to revoke a non-EEA deportation order, but legal advisors will need to secure full instructions in relation to the criminality of the individual concerned, their family and the impact deportation will have / is likely to have before providing comprehensive advice. It will also be necessary to carefully review the reasons why the deportation order was made, so all Home Office and Tribunal decisions must be secured.

If a revocation application is successful and the foreign criminal is outside of the UK, they will be able to apply for entry clearance to return to the UK under the Immigration Rules. The suitability and general grounds for refusal will need to be carefully considered; even if the deportation order isn't in force, the Home Office could still refuse entry.

If the application is successful and the Applicant remains in the UK, the permission to stay they held prior to the deportation order being issued will not be resurrected. Rather, the Home Office will decide what leave to issue them. I have seen cases where just 6 months permission to stay is issued at any one time, and others where 2.5 years (previously 3 years) leave is issued. The individual will need to continue to extend their leave in-time and in accordance with Rules/guidance until they have completed ten years continuous lawful residence, which is when they should hopefully be eligible to apply for indefinite leave to remain.

Unless the revocation application was submitted prior to 10 November 2014 (which was when the Immigration Act 2014 came into force, amending appeal rights under the Nationality, Immigration and Asylum Act 2002), a decision to refuse to revoke a deportation order itself will not attract a right of appeal. However, it's likely that an application to revoke a deportation order will include representations in relation to a protection or human rights claim, so any decision to refuse the protection or human rights claim would attract a right of appeal, unless certified as clearly unfounded.

EEA

Your client may be able to benefit from the EEA Regulations if the deportation order was made before 1 January 2021 under the EEA Regulations 2016, or if the order was issued after 1 January 2021, but in accordance with the 2016 Regulations (i.e. pre 31 December 2020 criminal conduct). This is in accordance with Schedule 2 of the Consequential Regulations 2020. Regulation 34 will apply to these matters, and Regulation 17 of the Frontier Workers Regulation 2020 will apply to frontier workers who want to consider revoking their deportation order.

Remember that, to revoke a deportation order with reference to the EEA provisions, the original deportation decision must have been issued with reference to EEA law; EEA provisions will not apply if your client can benefit from EEA rules now, but the original deportation decision was not issued with reference the EEA Regulations.

Under Regulation 34, the Secretary of State will consider revoking a deportation order if there has been a material change in circumstances. It can only be revoked if the individual who is subject to the order is outside of the UK. The Secretary of State must revoke the order if she believes that material change in circumstances means that the reasons why the order was made no longer apply. She must issue her decision within six months of receiving the application.

Succeeding with a revocation application will undoubtedly depend on the reasons why the deportation order was issued in the first place. Advisors should, therefore, review the Home Office's reasons for issuing the decision and any relevant Tribunal determinations before providing advice about the revocation procedure.

In our opinion, the following are relevant to a revocation application and should be considered when securing instructions and providing advice:

- Whether the Secretary of State / Tribunal applied the correct legal test when considering deportation. For example, did the higher threshold of serious or imperative grounds exist? In this case, the revocation application would need to be accompanied by extensive evidence to prove that the higher thresholds apply.

- Did the entire conduct pre-date 23:00 GMT on 31 December 2020, meaning the public policy, public security and public health test applies, yet the Secretary of State solely considered the conducive grounds test?

- Having assessed the evidence, do grounds exist to justify the initial deportation and continued exclusion from the UK? Was the Home Office/Tribunal correct to conclude that public policy, public security or public health grounds exist, or did they fail to consider relevant information or evidence about the individual or their circumstances?

- Has the applicant's risk of re-offending decreased, and can evidence of this be provided to prove their presence in the UK poses no risk? This could include an updated assessment, evidence of rehabilitative work undertaken after the previous decision(s).

- Other factors relevant to the individual can also be relied upon, for example, their age, health, strength of connections with the UK etc.

A successful revocation application will enable the individual to apply to return to the UK under the Immigration Rules. The individual will have commenced UK residence pre-31 December 2020, so Appendix EU may apply, although it may be difficult for the individual to meet the definition of a relevant EEA citizen in order to qualify for pre-settled status. This is because their continuous residence – which commenced prior to 31 December 2020 – may have been broken due to their custodial sentence or possible long absence from the UK. The deportation decision is also an event which can break continuous residence, although Appendix EU confirms that such a decision will not break continuous residence if it has been set aside or no longer has effect. This should, therefore, enable a client who has been deported from the UK to potentially return under Appendix EU, if they qualify for entry either as a result of their own residence in the UK or potentially on the basis of their relationship with someone else.

If the Secretary of State refuses the application to revoke the deportation order, an out of country right of appeal will exist under Regulation 37(1)(d) of the 2016 EEA Regulations. Unlike the appeals procedure for the initial deportation order, the individual will not have a right to return to the UK to make appeal submissions in person. If the application is a repeat application, or grounds raised were previously considered as part of the initial making of the deportation order, it is open to the Secretary of State to certify aspects of the decision. This will mean that the ground certified cannot form the basis of an appeal.

APPENDIX A

CHECKLIST – TAKING INSTRUCTIONS

- *Checklist relating to instructions to secure from EU client*
    - Date of birth.
    - Nationality; when/how did they acquire EU citizenship?
    - When did they first arrive in the UK?
    - Information relating to birth, parents' birth/nationality – do they have a claim to British citizenship?
    - Have they been issued a registration certificate or permanent residence under the EEA Regulations, or perhaps limited/indefinite leave to remain under Appendix EU?
    - What have they done since arriving in the UK? It is no longer necessary to prove that the individual has continuously undertaken a qualifying activity, but it would be useful to provide a background of their activities, in the hope you can prove that the offence is out of character.
    - Have they resided in the UK continuously since their arrival, or has their continuous residence been broken by way of absences outside of the UK (see Regulation 3 of the 2016 Regulations and Appendix EU of the Immigration Rules)?
    - What evidence can we provide to prove their continuous residence? Evidence could include: passports, payslips, HMRC records, bank statements, contract of employment, letters from employers/doctors/dentists, utility bills, tenancy agreements etc.
    - Details of the offence which resulted in the commencement of deportation proceedings (date of

offence, date of sentencing, length of sentence, did they plead guilty etc.).

- o Have they accepted responsibility for the offence? (remember this is not an opportunity to re-hear their criminal case).
- o Have they taken any steps to reduce likelihood of reoffending – any courses while in custody?
- o Pre-sentence report exist?
- o Criminal history – is this their first and only offence, or have they been convicted of any other offences in the UK/outside of the UK?
- o Ties to the UK – partner, children, family, friends etc?
- o Reasons why doesn't want to leave the UK.

- ***Instructions to secure from non-EU client***

  - o Nationality, date of birth.
  - o When did they first arrive in the UK?
  - o How did they arrive in the UK – legally or clandestinely?
  - o Have they ever held lawful status in the UK? If so, what status was held, why.
  - o Information relating to birth, parents' birth/nationality – do they have a claim to British citizenship?
  - o What have they done since arriving in the UK – employment, studies etc?
  - o Have they resided in the UK continuously since their arrival, or has their continuous residence been broken by way of absences outside of the UK?
  - o What evidence can we provide to prove their continuous residence? Evidence could include: passports, payslips, HMRC records, bank statements, contract of employment, letters from employers/doctors/dentists, utility bills, tenancy agreements etc.

- Details of the offence which resulted in the commencement of deportation proceedings (date of offence, date of sentencing, length of sentence, did they plead guilty etc.)
- Have they accepted responsibility for the offence?
- Have they taken any steps to reduce likelihood of reoffending – any courses while in custody?
- Pre-sentence report exist?
- Criminal history – is this their first and only offence, or have they been convicted of any other offences in the UK/outside of the UK?
- Ties to the UK – partner, children, family, friends etc?
- Reasons why doesn't want to leave the UK, including information about potential asylum grounds.

APPENDIX B

LIST OF DOCUMENTS TO SUPPORT REPRESENTATIONS / APPEALS

1. All representatives will need the initial decision to make a deportation order, and any relevant Tribunal decisions
2. Full disclosure of your client's criminality
3. Any Pre-Sentence Reports or OASys reports – these can be secured by contacting the Probation Service, and also by submitting a Subject Access Request to the Ministry of Justice
4. All courses / rehabilitation programmes completed by the offender since the conduct in question – these may be referenced in the Ministry of Justice disclosure, but the individual may have undertaken additional courses – perhaps to enhance employability – of their own accord
5. Witness statement from the individual concerned – this should comment on the life they have established in the UK, their acceptance of their wrongdoing, whether they express any sympathy and understanding of their offending, what they've learnt from their time in custody, how custody/removal has affected them and their family, the life / support system in the UK compared to what exists in their country of nationality
6. Witness statements from the individual's family, friends, professional acquaintances – these should comment on the individual's change of character, acceptance of their offending, whether they think the individual is sorry for their criminal history, will offend again, how they've coped during time apart, whether any children have been affected
7. Independent social worker report, to comment on the family's wellbeing while apart. This is especially important if children are

involved, and could help to comply with the unduly harsh test under the Immigration Rules

8. Psychological report, to comment on current risk of reoffending / risk to the public in the UK
9. Medical reports to comment on the individual / family's health, and whether this deteriorated due to temporary separation (while in custody) or following deportation
10. Documents relating to any children – school records, to comment on a possible change of behaviour while apart from the family member, medical reports, their own thoughts (if they're old enough, of course)
11. Documents relating to long residence / immigration history in the UK
12. For EEA cases – evidence of qualifying activity and continuity of residence

APPENDIX C

TEMPLATE APPEAL SKELETON ARGUMENT (SENTENCE 12 MONTHS – 4 YEARS)

IN THE FIRST TIER TRIBUNAL **Appeal no:**

IMMIGRATION AND ASYLUM CHAMBER

BETWEEN

XXXX

Appellant

and

SECRETARY OF STATE FOR THE HOME DEPARTMENT

Respondent

SKELETON ARGUMENT

Factual background

1. The Appellant (A) is a national of, born on…

2. Include information about the decision / offending / brief summary about why deportation is challenged.

Legal basis for deportation

3. By section 3(5)(a) of the Immigration Act 1971, A (as a person who is not a British citizen) is liable to deportation from the UK if R deems A's deportation to be conducive to the public good. Under section 32 of UK Borders Act 2007, A's custodial sentence has automatically triggered R's consideration of deportation proceedings; section 32 requires the deportation of a foreign criminal who has been sentenced to a term of at least 12 months' imprisonment. Section 32 is however subject to the exceptions set out in section 33 of the Act.

4. For the purpose of these proceedings, A seeks to rely on Exception 1 of section 33: *Exception 1 is where removal of the foreign criminal in pursuance of the deportation order would breach – (a) a person's Convention rights, …*

5. A submits that his deportation from the UK would amount to an unlawful breach of his Article 8 right to respect for his private and family life. A additionally submits that the Article 8 rights of his UK family, including minor children, will be disproportionately affected.

6. The Nationality, Immigration and Asylum Act 2002 makes specific provision in relation to the consideration of Article 8 in circumstances such as A's. Section 117A(b) provides that in cases concerning the deportation of foreign criminals, the considerations listed in section 117C must be taken into account.

7. Section 117C establishes a series of principles with are material to the determination of this appeal:

117C Article 8: additional considerations in cases involving foreign criminals

(1) The deportation of foreign criminals is in the public interest.

(2) The more serious the offence committed by the foreign criminal, the greater is the public interest in deportation of the criminal.

(3) In the case of a foreign criminal ("C") who has not been sentenced to a period of imprisonment of four years or more, the public interest requires C's deportation unless Exception 1 or Exception 2 applies.

(4) Exception 1 applies where—

(a) C has been lawfully resident in the United Kingdom for most of C's life,

(b) C is socially and culturally integrated in the United Kingdom, and

(c) there would be very significant obstacles to C's integration into the country to which C is proposed to be deported.

(5) Exception 2 applies where C has a genuine and subsisting relationship with a qualifying partner, or a genuine and subsisting parental relationship with a qualifying child, and the effect of C's deportation on the partner or child would be unduly harsh.

8. In the event that an appellant cannot satisfy the exceptions contained in the NIAA 2002, the Immigration Rules provide further detail on the appropriate approach to take when assessing whether deportation of an individual will be proportionate in the context of their wider circumstances, at paragraphs 398-399C:

398. Where a person claims that their deportation would be contrary to the UK's obligations under Article 8 of the Human Rights convention, and

> …
>
> *(b) the deportation of the person from the UK is conducive to the public good and in the public interest because they have been convicted of an offence for which they have been sentenced to a period of imprisonment of less than 4 years but at least 12 months;*
>
> …
>
> *The Secretary of State in assessing that claim will consider whether paragraph 399 or 399A applies and, if it does not, the public interest in deportation will only be outweighed by other factors where there are very compelling circumstances over and above those described in paragraphs 399 and 399A.*
>
> *399. This paragraph applies where paragraph 398 (b) … applies if–*
>
> *(a) the person has a genuine and subsisting parental relationship with a child under the age of 18 years who is in the UK, and*
>
> *(i) the child is a British Citizen…*
>
> *… and…*
>
> *(a) It would be unduly harsh for the child to live in the country to which the person is to be deported; and*
>
> *(b) It would be unduly harsh for the child to remain in the UK without the person who is to be deported; or*
>
> *(b) the person has a genuine and subsisting relationship with a partner who is in the UK and is a British Citizen or settled in the UK, and*
>
> *(i) the relationship was formed at a time when the person (deportee) was in the UK lawfully and their immigration status was not precarious; and*

> *(ii) it would be unduly harsh for that partner to live in the country to which the person is to be deported, because of compelling circumstances over and above those described in paragraph EX.2 of Appendix FM; and*
>
> *(iii) it would be unduly harsh for that partner to remain in the UK without the person who is to be deported.*

Application of law to facts

9. A's offending in the UK began in XX when A was aged XX.

10. …

11. A submits that it would be unduly harsh for his partner or their children to leave the UK in order to accompany A to XX. Evidence is provided of the challenging circumstances in XX, specifically in relation to issues such as access to education and healthcare, personal safety and security, and attitudes towards women and girls. XX would be forced to move to a country with a very different culture and standard of living from the UK; they would lose many of the advantages of their British citizenship. In addition, the children would lose their relationship with their maternal grandparents and extended family members. The best interests of XX and the children are served by their continued residence in the UK. R has not so far asserted that it would be reasonable for the children to leave the UK for residence elsewhere in the world. As a result, it is respectfully submitted that the primary issue for this tribunal is whether it would be unduly harsh for XXX to remain living in the UK without A as a member of their household.

12. On 4 September 2020, the Court of Appeal decision in **HA (Iraq) v SSHD [2020] WECA 1176** was handed down. This decision specifically considers deportation where the deportee has children who will be remaining in the UK, making useful findings concerning how a tribunal should assess whether

disruption caused by deportation would be *unduly harsh*, and how combinations of factors can lead to a decision to deport being disproportionate in the overall context of an individual case.

13. A has several convictions, and has received a custodial sentence which engaged the automatic deportation provisions. A has not however received a sentence exceeding 4 years, which would elevate the nature of the test to be applied in this appeal. As a result, A can be considered a 'medium offender' under the wording adopted by Underhill LJ in **HA (Iraq)**; "*…The statutory intention is evidently that the hurdle representing the unacceptable impact on a partner or child should be set somewhere between the (low) level applying in the case of persons who are liable to ordinary immigration removal (see Lord Carnwath's reference to section 117B (6) at the start of para. 23) and the (very high) level applying to serious offenders.*" [para 52]

14. At para 56 of the judgment, Underhill LJ said as follows:

> *…As explained above, the test under section 117C (5) does indeed require an appellant to establish a degree of harshness going beyond a threshold "acceptable" level. It is not necessarily wrong to describe that as an "ordinary" level of harshness, and I note that Lord Carnwath did not jib at UTJ Southern's use of that term. However, I think the Appellants are right to point out that it may be misleading if used incautiously. There seems to be me to be two (related) risks. First, "ordinary" is capable of being understood as meaning anything which is not exceptional, or in any event rare. That is not the correct approach: see para. 52 above. There is no reason in principle why cases of "undue" harshness my not occur quite commonly. Secondly, if tribunals treat the essential question as being "is this level of harshness out of the ordinary?" they may be tempted to find that Exemption 2 does not apply simply on the basis that the situation fits into some commonly-encountered pattern. That would be dangerous. How a child will be affected by a parents' deportation will depend on*

> *an almost infinitely variable range of circumstances and it is not possible to identify a baseline of "ordinariness"...*

15. ...

16. When striking the proportionality balance, it is relevant and appropriate to consider that A's sentence was the minimum level for him to qualify as a foreign criminal (**HA (Iraq)**, para 90). Underhill LJ recorded the following findings at paras. 92 and 95:

> *...The question then arises whether it cuts both ways – that is, whether in principle a potential deportee can rely, as part of the overall proportionality assessment, on the fact that his offence was at or near the bottom of the scale of seriousness. It seems to me that this must indeed be the case... Since it was established in KO that the relative seriousness of the offence cannot be taken into account in considering Exception 2 (see para. 43 above), it must be capable of being deployed by the potential deportee at the second stage.*
>
> *...If the UT were to regard HA as only having failed by a small margin to bring himself within Exception 2 and/or if there were other circumstances, weighing against deportation, the fact that his offence, as measured by his sentence, had been near the bottom of the scale of seriousness might make a material difference to how the balance was struck.*

17. A does not seek to argue that his offending is inconsequential; he undoubtedly made mistakes with his conduct as a younger man. Nevertheless, A has rehabilitated since the commission of offences in XX. He was released from custody in XX and in the intervening XX months has committed to living in accordance with the law. Such rehabilitation is a valid consideration for the tribunal, as per para 141 of **HA (Iraq)**:

> *That those authorities seem to me to establish is that the fact that a potential deportee has shown positive evidence of rehabilitation, and thus of a reduced risk of re-offending, cannot*

> *be excluded from the overall proportionately exercise. The authorities say so, and it must be right in principle in view of the holistic nature of that exercise...*

18. A has no valuable experience of living in XX, having spent only a total of XX years in the country between birth and the age of XX. By contrast, he has lived in the UK for over XX years, having entered with indefinite leave. He completed his formative teenage years in the UK, and the most important connections of his life are here through his partner and children.

19. It would be unduly harsh on A's children and partner to deport A from the UK given the children's young age, the importance of A within the household, and the strength of the bond between the appellant and his family. In the event that the tribunal is not minded to agree that Exception 2 is satisfied in this case, the combination of factors in A's case – his family relationships, the duration of his UK residence, his good conduct since release from custody, the relatively low level of offending – together outweigh the public interest and the appeal should be allowed.

MORE BOOKS BY LAW BRIEF PUBLISHING

A selection of our other titles available now:-

'A Practical Guide to Solicitor and Client Costs – 2nd Edition' by Robin Dunne
'Constructive Dismissal – Practice Pointers and Principles' by Benjimin Burgher
'A Practical Guide to Religion and Belief Discrimination Claims in the Workplace' by Kashif Ali
'A Practical Guide to the Law of Medical Treatment Decisions' by Ben Troke
'Fundamental Dishonesty and QOCS in Personal Injury Proceedings: Law and Practice' by Jake Rowley
'A Practical Guide to the Law in Relation to School Exclusions' by Charlotte Hadfield & Alice de Coverley
'A Practical Guide to Divorce for the Silver Separators' by Karin Walker
'The Right to be Forgotten – The Law and Practical Issues' by Melissa Stock
'A Practical Guide to Planning Law and Rights of Way in National Parks, the Broads and AONBs' by James Maurici QC, James Neill et al
'A Practical Guide to Election Law' by Tom Tabori
'A Practical Guide to the Law in Relation to Surrogacy' by Andrew Powell
'A Practical Guide to Claims Arising from Fatal Accidents – 2nd Edition' by James Patience
'A Practical Guide to the Ownership of Employee Inventions – From Entitlement to Compensation' by James Tumbridge & Ashley Roughton
'A Practical Guide to Asbestos Claims' by Jonathan Owen & Gareth McAloon
'A Practical Guide to Stamp Duty Land Tax in England and Northern Ireland' by Suzanne O'Hara
'A Practical Guide to the Law of Farming Partnerships' by Philip Whitcomb

'Covid-19, Homeworking and the Law – The Essential Guide to Employment and GDPR Issues' by Forbes Solicitors
'Covid-19, Force Majeure and Frustration of Contracts – The Essential Guide' by Keith Markham
'Covid-19 and Criminal Law – The Essential Guide' by Ramya Nagesh
'Covid-19 and Family Law in England and Wales – The Essential Guide' by Safda Mahmood
'A Practical Guide to the Law of Unlawful Eviction and Harassment – 2nd Edition' by Stephanie Lovegrove
'Covid-19, Residential Property, Equity Release and Enfranchisement – The Essential Guide' by Paul Sams and Louise Uphill
'Covid-19, Brexit and the Law of Commercial Leases – The Essential Guide' by Mark Shelton
'A Practical Guide to Costs in Personal Injury Claims – 2nd Edition' by Matthew Hoe
'A Practical Guide to the General Data Protection Regulation (GDPR) – 2nd Edition' by Keith Markham
'Ellis on Credit Hire – Sixth Edition' by Aidan Ellis & Tim Kevan
'A Practical Guide to Working with Litigants in Person and McKenzie Friends in Family Cases' by Stuart Barlow
'Protecting Unregistered Brands: A Practical Guide to the Law of Passing Off' by Lorna Brazell
'A Practical Guide to Secondary Liability and Joint Enterprise Post-Jogee' by Joanne Cecil & James Mehigan
'A Practical Guide to the Pre-Action RTA Claims Protocol for Personal Injury Lawyers' by Antonia Ford
'A Practical Guide to Neighbour Disputes and the Law' by Alexander Walsh
'A Practical Guide to Forfeiture of Leases' by Mark Shelton
'A Practical Guide to Coercive Control for Legal Practitioners and Victims' by Rachel Horman

'A Practical Guide to Rights Over Airspace and Subsoil' by Daniel Gatty

'Tackling Disclosure in the Criminal Courts – A Practitioner's Guide' by Narita Bahra QC & Don Ramble

'A Practical Guide to the Law of Driverless Cars – Second Edition' by Alex Glassbrook, Emma Northey & Scarlett Milligan

'A Practical Guide to TOLATA Claims' by Greg Williams

'Artificial Intelligence – The Practical Legal Issues' by John Buyers

'A Practical Guide to the Law of Prescription in Scotland' by Andrew Foyle

'A Practical Guide to the Construction and Rectification of Wills and Trust Instruments' by Edward Hewitt

'A Practical Guide to the Law of Bullying and Harassment in the Workplace' by Philip Hyland

'How to Be a Freelance Solicitor: A Practical Guide to the SRA-Regulated Freelance Solicitor Model' by Paul Bennett

'A Practical Guide to Prison Injury Claims' by Malcolm Johnson

'A Practical Guide to the Small Claims Track' by Dominic Bright

'A Practical Guide to Advising Clients at the Police Station' by Colin Stephen McKeown-Beaumont

'A Practical Guide to Antisocial Behaviour Injunctions' by Iain Wightwick

'Practical Mediation: A Guide for Mediators, Advocates, Advisers, Lawyers, and Students in Civil, Commercial, Business, Property, Workplace, and Employment Cases' by Jonathan Dingle with John Sephton

'The Mini-Pupillage Workbook' by David Boyle

'A Practical Guide to Crofting Law' by Brian Inkster

'A Practical Guide to Spousal Maintenance' by Liz Cowell

'A Practical Guide to the Law of Domain Names and Cybersquatting' by Andrew Clemson

'A Practical Guide to the Law of Gender Pay Gap Reporting' by Harini Iyengar

'A Practical Guide to the Rights of Grandparents in Children Proceedings' by Stuart Barlow
'NHS Whistleblowing and the Law' by Joseph England
'Employment Law and the Gig Economy' by Nigel Mackay & Annie Powell
'A Practical Guide to Noise Induced Hearing Loss (NIHL) Claims' by Andrew Mckie, Ian Skeate, Gareth McAloon
'An Introduction to Beauty Negligence Claims – A Practical Guide for the Personal Injury Practitioner' by Greg Almond
'Intercompany Agreements for Transfer Pricing Compliance' by Paul Sutton
'Zen and the Art of Mediation' by Martin Plowman
'A Practical Guide to the SRA Principles, Individual and Law Firm Codes of Conduct 2019 – What Every Law Firm Needs to Know' by Paul Bennett
'A Practical Guide to Adoption for Family Lawyers' by Graham Pegg
'A Practical Guide to Industrial Disease Claims' by Andrew Mckie & Ian Skeate
'A Practical Guide to Redundancy' by Philip Hyland
'A Practical Guide to Vicarious Liability' by Mariel Irvine
'A Practical Guide to Applications for Landlord's Consent and Variation of Leases' by Mark Shelton
'A Practical Guide to Relief from Sanctions Post-Mitchell and Denton' by Peter Causton
'A Practical Guide to Equity Release for Advisors' by Paul Sams
'A Practical Guide to the Law Relating to Food' by Ian Thomas
'A Practical Guide to Financial Services Claims' by Chris Hegarty
'The Law of Houses in Multiple Occupation: A Practical Guide to HMO Proceedings' by Julian Hunt
'A Practical Guide to Unlawful Eviction and Harassment' by Stephanie Lovegrove
'Occupiers, Highways and Defective Premises Claims: A Practical Guide Post-Jackson – 2nd Edition' by Andrew Mckie

‘A Practical Guide to Financial Ombudsman Service Claims’ by Adam Temple & Robert Scrivenor
'A Practical Guide to Advising Schools on Employment Law' by Jonathan Holden
‘A Practical Guide to Running Housing Disrepair and Cavity Wall Claims: 2nd Edition’ by Andrew Mckie & Ian Skeate
‘A Practical Guide to Holiday Sickness Claims – 2nd Edition’ by Andrew Mckie & Ian Skeate
‘Arguments and Tactics for Personal Injury and Clinical Negligence Claims’ by Dorian Williams
‘A Practical Guide to Drone Law’ by Rufus Ballaster, Andrew Firman, Eleanor Clot
‘A Practical Guide to Compliance for Personal Injury Firms Working With Claims Management Companies’ by Paul Bennett
‘A Practical Guide to Dog Law for Owners and Others’ by Andrea Pitt
‘RTA Allegations of Fraud in a Post-Jackson Era: The Handbook – 2nd Edition’ by Andrew Mckie
‘RTA Personal Injury Claims: A Practical Guide Post-Jackson’ by Andrew Mckie
‘On Experts: CPR35 for Lawyers and Experts’ by David Boyle
‘An Introduction to Personal Injury Law’ by David Boyle
‘A Practical Guide to Subtle Brain Injury Claims’ by Pankaj Madan

These books and more are available to order online direct from the publisher at www.lawbriefpublishing.com, where you can also read free sample chapters. For any queries, contact us on 0844 587 2383 or mail@lawbriefpublishing.com.

Our books are also usually in stock at www.amazon.co.uk with free next day delivery for Prime members, and at good legal bookshops such as Wildy & Sons.

We are regularly launching new books in our series of practical day-to-day practitioners' guides. Visit our website and join our free newsletter to be kept informed and to receive special offers, free chapters, etc.

You can also follow us on Twitter at www.twitter.com/lawbriefpub.

www.ingramcontent.com/pod-product-compliance
Lightning Source LLC
LaVergne TN
LVHW022112200926
848481LV00003B/1145
* 9 7 8 1 9 1 3 7 1 5 1 6 8 *